CREATIVE PREACHING
AND
ORAL WRITING

Richard Carl Hoefler

CREATIVE PREACHING AND ORAL WRITING

ISBN 0-89536-349-6   PRINTED IN U.S.A.

TABLE OF CONTENTS

Appendix

Dedicated to the student body

of the Lutheran Theological

Southern Seminary

Preface

We begin not with a defense of preaching but a definition, for how can you defend an act of foolishness, as Paul describes preaching in the first four chapters of 1 Corinthians. "God," says Paul, "decided to save those who believe, by means of the foolish message we preach." But it is a foolishness that is "wiser than wise men's wisdom." It is a weakness that is "stronger than men's strength."

The strength of preaching is God's power, not ours. Paul says, "We do not speak in words taught by human wisdom, but in words taught by the Spirit." The proclamation of Christ crucified is "the power of God and the wisdom of God." The Word forgives, redeems, reconciles, and gives new life. Therefore, the ultimate test of preaching is not what the sermon says, but what it does. Preaching is creative.

The following twelve statements are not a complete definition of preaching, but a starting definition. It is where we begin. Ultimately preaching can be defined only by the people in the pew. When they identify with the words of the sermon, become involved in them, and are changed by them, that is preaching. When God speaks and people hear and are moved to act in a new way, that is preaching — creative preaching.

A Starting Definition for Preaching

1. Preaching is the proclamation of the gospel — telling the good news of what God has done, is doing, and will do. It is not talking about God, but it is the means, in each generation by which God speaks to the people. Preaching is not a person revealing God and truths about him. It is God disclosing himself and speaking of himself through a chosen witness.

2. Preaching is biblical, based on thorough exegetical study and interpretation of the Bible — the Bible's own

message, not a use of the Bible for our purposes or to support our preconceived ideas.

3. The content of preaching is bifocal, concerned both with the needs of God and with the needs of people. It is centered, as God's Word is centered, in Jesus Christ seen as God's redemptive act, the divine event. At the same time it is directed, as God's Word is directed, to the invasion of common life to restore a broken relationship between the Creator and the created, to establish a new option for human freedom and dignity, and to bring all creation to the fulfillment of its intended destiny.

4. Such preaching is itself part of God's redemptive act in Christ. In such preaching, God's act of redemption takes place in the here and now. It is not simply remembered, but made present.

5. The content of preaching is seldom congenial with the thought and cultural habits of the times, but rather is in collision with them. It comes to question, to challenge all we are, including the preacher, and is met by resistance and counterattack. It proclaims a word that punishes as well as pardons, and in most cases disturbs and troubles before it can heal.

6. The end of preaching is always positive. It faces the reality of sin, guilt, and estrangement frankly, but to the end that it might, because of God's forgiveness and mercy, proclaim the gift of new life to people. The primary thrust of preaching is to tell persons who they are now and what they can do now because of what God has done through the life, death, and resurrection of Jesus Christ.

7. Preaching is built on the conviction that the living God is redemptively at work in this world. It proclaims what God has done in the past to bring people to an awareness of what God is doing now, to the end that persons surrender themselves to this living God to be used by him in his continuous contemporary redemptive action.

8. Preaching is a unique kind of speaking, of language. It is like no other form of communication. It is a dialogue made possible bv the work of the Holy Spirit, a dialogue between God and people in which the preacher remains a hearer while speaking God's word. The preacher is not over against the congregation; he is part of the listening congregation.

9. The method of preaching is to make visual that which is abstract and obtuse. It does not enlarge the Word of God, but enlightens the listeners so that they might hear the Word of God. It strives to eliminate, insofar as possible, the hindrances to clear understanding of the Word of God, so that people might acknowledge their need for God and respond to God with love and trust.

10. The purpose of preaching is to bring persons to the place where they will act as if what God says is true. It is not to convince the listeners of the truth, beyond all doubt, but to bring them to the place where they will act on the truth, despite doubts.

11. Preaching is never ambitious to eliminate the element of mystery in revelation. It respects the ultimate sovereignty of God and is concerned to proclaim only that which God desires to reveal of himself. This means that the gospel which the preacher proclaims is always greater than the preacher's understanding of it.

12. Preaching calls individuals out from the world, feeds and unites them, and then sends them forth as the church to be God's living body in a needy and empty world. It celebrates the joy of love's victory over hate, life's victory over death, and God's ultimate victory over all the destructive rebellion within his kingdom.

1

Attitude Determines Action

Let us begin with something vital to effective preaching, yet frequently neglected — attitude. For the speaker, words are the tools needed to convey ideas. But behind each word spoken is an attitude. Attitude determines how successful words will be in communicating the exact meaning of ideas. What a person says will be colored by how he feels about what is being said. The words chosen may be right, but they will fail to communicate accurately unless the attitude agrees with the ideas the words are meant to express.

If a man is asked his opinion, and answers his wife, "Yes, honey, that dress looks real great on you," the way in which he says these words will determine whether or not she wears it or hangs it in the closet until she gives it away. This is part of the uniqueness of oral communication. We communicate not only by what we say, but by the *way* we say it. We convey meaning by the inflections and tonal quality of the voice. And this is determined in most cases by attitude.

I once had a professor of preaching who told us that we should boldly proclaim judgment and the wrath of God, but should always do it with "tears in your hearts." That does make a difference. Some preachers tell people that they are going to Hell, and you can tell by the way they say it that they get a sense of perverted pleasure from being in a position where they can get back at the world through you. Others talk about sin as a healthy person talks about disease, rather than as a condition by which the speaker himself is infected and shares the symptoms. It all depends on attitude — the way he says it, the facial expressions and bodily gestures that accompany the words.

Words are important — the correct word, the clear word — but behind words are attitudes that ultimately will decide what will be communicated. Yet, interestingly enough, this is seldom dealt with when preaching is discussed.

There are four basic categories of attitudes that should be considered: the attitude toward the preaching task in general; the attitude of the speaker toward the content; the speaker's attitude toward himself or herself; the speaker's attitude toward the listeners.

Attitude Toward the Task of Preaching

Many people enter the pulpit with the attitude that it is a performance which they must do well to receive the silent applause of satisfied parishioners. The ultimate goal is the warm handshake at the door and those ego-building words, "That was a great sermon this morning, Pastor," or, "That was one of the best sermons I have ever heard." There is nothing wrong with satisfied and complimentary listeners. Over the years, this is what keeps us going when we wonder if what we do is really worth the effort. But this is the bonus for good preaching, not the basis of it. It can be a dangerous mis-directive and motivate us to strive for approval before, and above, everything else. So often, if this is the attitude, when the time comes for courageous and prophetic preaching born within the demands of the text itself, the preacher will be ill-equipped to meet the challenge.

As we shall point out in the body of this book, there is a need for fresh expression when we speak the Word of God, but we should not strive for freshness to impress the listeners with our profound insights into the gospel and our skills as public speakers. Rather, we strive for freshness that the Word might become alive in the lives of our listeners.

The test of good preaching is not our reputation as a speaker, but the response preaching brings about in the lives of our listeners. There have been many good sermons that have ended up being good — good for nothing, because nothing ever came of them. Nothing ever happened in the life of the congregation because of the sermon. Our attitude should not be first, "I am going to impress these people with a splendid performance of the Word," but, "I am going to express the Word as clearly as possible." For, if anything is ever to happen because of *our* preaching, it will depend on *his* Word.

Our basic attitude toward the task of preaching should be built on a sound theology of the Word, a theology that teaches that the Word, in and of itself, is efficacious. When the Word is set free from the written page and becomes vocal, something happens. It possesses a unique power. The Word not only *announces* forgiveness, redemption, and the new life of faith, but *produces* it. This means that, when the Word is absent, there is no faith, For there is no faith in silence.

Students frequently come to me when faced with an assignment of preaching in the seminary chapel. Their attitude is, "What can I say that is new and fresh to seminary professors and to upper class students who know far more about the Scripture than I do?" They are defeated by their attitude before they enter the pulpit. Nerves take over. They panic. "What am I doing here anyway?" "I've got to get out of this place!" But it is too late. Escape now would be more personally damaging than failure. So they accompany their nerves into the pulpit.

When I see this beginning to happen, I try to make it clear that the task of preaching is not to impress but express. When you enter the pulpit, think of little else than "Preach the Word, for the Word has the power to do all the rest." No matter how much professors or students know about the Scriptures, without a vocal witness to them personally, they cannot possess a vital and living faith. For faith is not an individual intellectual thing which people possess. It is a shared experience of the community. No person can have faith for another. But it is equally true that no person can have faith without another. We need the face-to-face witness of each other to keep our own faith vital and alive. That is why the church was established, not first to worship God, but to be a place where people might hear the Word of God. And that is why a congregation calls a speaker to stand in the pulpit on Sunday morning, to assure each person who comes to worship that the Word of God will be made vocal in this fellowship.

Therefore, as we enter the pulpit, our attitude should be that the task ahead is to make the Word of God vocal and to proclaim that Word with clarity. The Word of God is power and it will work if we get out of the way.

This does not mean that the Word does everything and we do nothing. To get out of the way so that the Word might work is a real art that takes hard work and skillful effort. In the pulpit the Word is master and we are only servants. Trust the Word and its efficacious power.

This Word we are to trust is the gospel. It is the good news of what God has done for us in Jesus Christ. Therefore, it is a word of hope. It is a bit of good news in a world deafened by bad news. As we enter the pulpit we should remind ourselves that the people who look up at us have been, for the most part, beaten down by a week of troubles and frustrations. They have lived on the edge of raw nerves and short tempers.

Newspapers and TV have bombarded them with what's wrong with our world: Everything from red food coloring to cigarettes are potential cancer causers. . . . If the present birth rate continues, the sheer weight of the population will be greater than the total weight of the world. . . . The arms race is escalating. . . . Energy is being exhausted. . . . The crime rate is going up and the stock market is going down. . . . Taxes and prices are running a race to see which can climb the higher. . . . Unemployment **soars** and Social Security is nearly bankrupt.

From a world of this endless clamor of calamities and threats, our listeners come to us. The gospel we proclaim may be the only word of hope they will have heard all week, and it may well be the only word of hope they will hear in the week to come.

With this in mind, we enter the pulpit. Therefore, our attitude should be, if these people are ever to hear the gospel they must hear it from us now. Our attitude should be a sense of "urgent immediacy" about the Word we preach.

However, we are not to enter the pulpit with the attitude that the "immediacy of preaching" means that if the sermon is effective we are going to see an immediate and positive response. Preaching is not like salesmanship, where success depends upon people buying the product now. Preaching is more like farming. This gospel we proclaim is like a seed sown. When we are called to preach his Word, God does not promise us the satisfaction of seeing the end results of our efforts. We are called simply to plant. In God's time the seed will ripen and spring forth and grow toward the harvest.

Many young preachers soon become discouraged and develop a sour attitude toward preaching because miraculous things fail to happen as the result of their preaching. So they turn their attention and efforts to activities in the church which produce more immediate results. But such discouragement with the power of the pulpit is unfair to the potential of the Word. The working of the Word is not always dramatic and immediately appreciated, but it is the foundation on which all other activities of the church depend. In every age it has been the preached Word in the pulpit that has given to the church the power to exist and renew itself. It is the Word that enables the church to stand even against "the gates of Hell."

Therefore, enter the pulpit with the attitude that preaching is absolutely essential to the life of the church. The Word is not in competition with other activities of the church but enables all other activities of the church to function fully. It is the Word proclaimed publicly from the pulpit that gives birth to faith and nourishes it. It is the preached Word from the pulpit that equips the saints for their work both in the church and in the world. It is for the task of preaching that God establishes the church and this congregation, that at one place and time, this fellowship of believers might meet together and share the experience of publicly listening to what the Word God has to speak for this time to these people.

Attitude Toward Content

The preaching situation is unique as a public speaking activity, for it is a situation in which we not only speak but are spoken to. This is important in understanding the right attitude toward our content.

Some people convey the attitude in the pulpit that they are called prophets of God possessing a secret message from on high that is really too holy for our ears. Others stand in the pulpit like drill sergeants barking orders to raw recruits. Still others take on the appearance of profound scholars having emerged from the cloisters of their studies to share with the ignorant masses the gems of their scholarly research and wisdom. And then there are those who assume the attitude of tidy teachers about to talk to their little children and tell them how to be tidy, too. All such attitudes of superiority are deadly in the pulpit. The preacher becomes authoritarian and the Word loses its credibility as an authentic authority.

Our attitude toward content must first be that the sermon is a word to be shared. As speakers, we need to hear this message as well as our listeners. As someone has so aptly defined witnessing, "We are thirsty people telling other thirsty people where water can be found."

This means that we ourselves must be interested in what we have to say and concerned that it is important. We must have done our homework. We need to speak against a background of thorough research and personal involvement with the text. Security of content means self-struggle with the text. We need to be sure of what we are saying. Not that we know it all, but that what we do know, we know well. People soon sense when a speaker is stretching to fill up an allotted time in the pulpit. The content we bring into the pulpit should be but the top of the iceberg that was created in our study by our research and examination of the text.

We are not to take the attitude that we are on *top* of the text. Rather we are *in* the text and saturated with it. The gospel is always bigger than the one who attempts to proclaim it. There is a difference between getting hold of a text and having a text get a hold on us. It is the difference between giving the impression that we have *found* something and giving the impression that we are *finding* something. The right attitude toward the content of our sermon is "timely urgency." We must convey the attitude that, together with the listening congregation, we are discovering the meaning of God's Word for them and for us.

We need to give the *impression* that the sermon is not something worked out in the study last week, but it is something that is being lived, experienced in the pulpit now. The attitude of immediacy is essential as we deal with content.

This involves not only our mental attitude but the form and format of the sermon, the words we choose, and the way the sermon is delivered. The sermon is to be viewed not as something finished beforehand that is brought into the pulpit and given as a finished product to the listeners, but as a message which the speaker is going to create in the minds of the listeners. The sermon will be a cooperative venture. The listeners are going to participate with us as we deal with a text and discover its meaning. The listeners are not so much going to hear a sermon; they are going to *make* a sermon in their minds. Even though we will provide the words and the ideas of the sermon — words and ideas that we have carefully worked out beforehand — we must view the sermon as a product of the pulpit that can happen only while we are in the process of delivering it.

Our attitude toward the content of any sermon is an attitude not only of immediacy but of expectancy. We approach the content as something we are in the process of discovering; we are hearing God speak as well as speaking God's Word. We are at the same time the one who speaks and the one who is spoken to.

Attitude Toward Self

We often hear people say that they are going to take some speech training in order to better express themselves. It may come as a surprise, but self-expression can be the most damaging barrier for good communication, especially in the pulpit. For an approach to preaching as a speaking opportunity places the attention on self rather than on the listener. Good communication in the pulpit or anywhere else demands just the opposite. If the speaker is ever to communicate effectively, he needs to convince the listeners that, for him, in the shared experience of the sermon, they are the only people in the world. The speaker's attitude must convey total interest and complete concern for the listeners.

Many times the preacher uses the pulpit as an opportunity for personal therapy. Preachers vent their emotions and prejudices, ride their hobby-horses, champion their favorite causes, and attack their most hated targets. In this age of "letting-it-all-hang-out" and "personal authenticity," a captive audience and fifteen minutes of uninterrupted attention is too much to resist. So the speaker opens himself up and lets it all gush forth from the "load on his chest" to the "chip on his shoulder."

When such a sermon is finished, we know more than we ever wanted to know about the preacher, but very little about our Lord, the Christ.

There is little doubt that it is a great temptation, when we stand in the pulpit, "six feet above contradiction," to get back at the obstinate council member or the antagonistic church member who discredits everything we try to do. But, this is not only unfair and dishonest to those who cannot speak back; it is also a perversion of preaching, for it makes a personal platform out of a public pulpit.

Philips Brooks defined preaching as "truth through personality." But when self-expression becomes the basic attitude of the preacher toward the pulpit opportunity, little truth gets through. In the pulpit, the less attention directed to the individual personality of the speaker the better.

How, then, do we handle personal testimony in the pulpit? One answer is, "Very cautiously." Granted, personal testimony is important in the total picture of Christian witnessing. But there are, or at least there should be, more appropriate places for individual testimony than the public spotlight of the pulpit. For example, face-to-face encounters and group situations, where there is an opportunity for shared religious experiences, are far more fruitful settings for personal testimony. It has always impressed me that Matthew, Mark, Luke, and John could say so much about what Christ meant to them and, at the same time, say so little about themselves personally.

The pulpit situation is potentially dangerous for telling things about ourselves. The very architectural setting forces the focus of attention away from the many to the one. Because of this, personal testimony can easily degenerate into an autobiography about "How I succeeded in my attempt at personal sainthood." The preacher becomes not only the visual focus of attention; he becomes the main concern of the sermon. In some cases the preacher becomes the sermon. The medium becoming the message is not something we should strive for, but do all in our power to work against.

Karl Barth opened up the whole movement of 20th Century Theology with the profound discovery that when people come to church they do not want to hear what the preacher has to say, but what God has to say. It therefore follows that the correct attitude toward self is best expressed in the simple pulpit prayer, "Lord, let me get out of the way." In the pulpit, your and my first and only task is to proclaim Christ and him crucified, not what redemption means to me or how I came to be saved. It would be well if the entrance to every pulpit were marked by the words, "Sir, we would see Jesus."

We need also to remind ourselves that when we stand in the pulpit on the average Sunday morning, we face a congregation not of unbelievers but a congregation of redeemed, baptized Christians, the Body of Christ. It may be in the preacher's estimation a sick and ailing "body," but it is the Body of Christ nonetheless. On any given Sunday morning there will be people present with religious experiences and faith equal to, if not greater than, ours. If personal testimony is in order, it should be a shared testimony where everyone has an opportunity to respond with their own experiences. The ordinary preaching situation does not provide such a setting.

The pulpit is designed to hold the Word of God, only incidentally the preacher. The pulpit is not our personal platform; it belongs to God and his people. It is interesting that in the ancient inventories of church furnishing, pulpits are always listed as furniture of the nave rather than of the chancel. We need to remind ourselves that pulpits are raised not because of the prestige of the preaching profession, but in order that people might more easily hear the Word of God.

When we are privileged to occupy that elevated pulpit, it is not because of our own personal piety or our extraordinary spiritual experiences. Our right to stand in the pulpit is not that we are holy, but because, hopefully, we are wholly dedicated to the gospel. Luther politely puts us in our place when he points out that the efficacy of the Word is not dependent on the spiritual status of the speaker, but on the Word in and of itself. Enter the pulpit, therefore, with the attitude that there is a story to be told and that story is not about ourselves but about Jesus Christ.

Hence, we should avoid all such phrases as, "I believe," "I think," "It seems to me," and "In my opinion." Such phrases call undue and unnecessary attention to the speaker. It should be obvious that we would not be in this place, occupying this position in the pulpit, unless we believe what we preached. The accepted fact that we are ministers of the Word should be ample evidence that we are dedicated to and believe the Word we preach. If, by chance, some listener doubts our sincerity because of the way we live in the world, no amount of "I believe" phrases in the pulpit is going to convince him otherwise. The enthusiasm and conviction that marks the way we deliver the sermon is a far more effective means of conveying our personal commitment to the content of the sermon.

When entering the pulpit the correct attitude toward self should be neither self-expression nor personal testimony. Rather, it should be that we have been caught by a message that must be told, and are striving to get out of the way so that message can move through us as easily as possible and capture our listeners as it has captured us.

Attitude Toward the Listeners

Authenticity is essential in the pulpit. Not that we come across as an honest person, as much as we come across as one who is genuinely interested in and concerned about the views, needs, and interests of the listeners. The congregation needs to be assured that the preacher knows what he is talking about, but even more they need to be certain that the preacher knows he is speaking to them.

The preaching situation is a meeting of minds. It is a sharing of feelings. It is a dialogue of thought. True, the listeners do not respond vocally. They do not talk back to the preacher, but they can "react back" with facial and body gestures to communicate their feelings and thoughts.

We need to convey by our attitude that we are going out of ourselves to meet the listeners. We are giving ourselves to them and at the same time receiving from them. We need to convey a sensitivity to the thinking and the feelings of the listeners.

One of the ways we do this is to take every opportunity within the development of the content to stop to acknowledge the listeners. We can do this by the use of such phrases as, "You know what I mean," or, "You all have had the same experience," or, "This same problem faces us." These and similar phrases show that we are aware of the listeners and are vitally concerned that they see the connection between the content of the sermon and the struggle of their lives.

Many times the student preacher will say something humorous in the pulpit, and the congregation will respond with interrupting laughter. But the preacher doesn't even crack a smile. This is deadly. It cuts the speaker off from the listeners and destroys the sense of a shared experience. When a congregation laughs and the preacher doesn't, the listeners often feel they have done something wrong. They become uneasy and insecure with the speaker. As speakers, we should be sensitive to these situations and react to any response we get from the listeners. We need to do everything within our power to make of the preaching situation a dialogue of thought and feeling.

There are times when the material presented is obviously in opposition to the accepted beliefs and opinions of the listeners. We are perhaps giving a radically new interpretation to a familiar passage of Scripture that has long held a traditional interpretation. Here, especially, we need to convey to the listeners that we are genuinely concerned with their point of view. We understand why and how they hold the position they do, but we would appreciate their consideration of a new and different interpretation. Never attack or ridicule a position the listeners hold. Rather, invite them to reconsider their position in light of new evidence, or at least from a different perspective. In the pulpit, it is easy to win an argument and lose a congregation. The words of the sermon are the Word of God only when they are received in the lives of the listeners.

When you first enter the pulpit, you should look out at the people. Take time to *see* those in front and back and to the sides of you. Let them know you are aware that they are there. Say to yourself, "God loves these people, and so do I." If you fail to say anything at all that will be remembered, or that will mean anything permanent in the lives of the listeners, but at least convey the feeling that they are loved, you will not have wasted their time, or yours, in the pulpit.

As you stand in the pulpit waiting to begin, you should smile, or at least have a pleasant look on your face. This is true no matter what direction your sermon will eventually take. The tragic mistake of student preachers is that they are so serious about the content of their sermons that this seriousness comes across as antagonism. One of the most frequent reactions to a student preacher is, "Who is he mad at?"

Remember that, when they lowered the paralytic through the roof to the feet of Jesus, the first thing our Lord said to the man was, "Your sins are forgiven." In modern idiom this means, "God is not angry with you," or "God loves you." This was not only the beginning of healing and faith for that paralytic; it should be the beginning attitude of any Word God addresses to anyone.

We begin our sermon with the attitude that God loves each and every person present and pray that at the end of the sermon this will be the firm conviction of everyone who has heard the sermon.

Summary

In summary, we must convey the attitude that we are speaking a word of power. By making the Word vocal, we are making faith possible. In the content of our sermon, are sharing with our listeners the creation of a sermon. As we speak we are being spoken to. Our attitude toward self is that we must get out of the way and let God's Word come through. Our attitude toward our listeners is that we are fully aware of their presence, understand their needs, and we are concerned that they know that God loves them and so do we.

Postscript

It should be added that attitude does not *begin* in the pulpit. Our appearance, the neatness and appropriateness of our dress, the way we walk, the way we sit, the way we conduct the service and participate in it, get it over, and get out, that attitude will color all we have to say in the sermon. A speaker is not a voice, but a person. When we speak, the whole body speaks and conveys the message. It is important that everything work together to create a common and consistent message.

2

The Process of Sermon Creation

The moment of conception for a sermon may occur almost anyplace. It may happen while you are studying the Scripture, reading a book, driving a car, watching TV, or talking with another person. But it is at the preacher's desk that the sermon is born. It is what happens at this desk that is the concern of this chapter.

It is at the pastor's desk that the sermon is born. Not a desk isolated in some ivory tower, but a public desk loaded with work, located at the heart and nerve center of an active church in the midst of the world. It is about this desk that people gather, sometimes for a friendly chat, but often bringing with them consciences heavy with guilt, minds troubled by conflicting desires, nerves rubbed raw by a harsh and indifferent world. It is to this desk that telephone calls come — some irritating, some urgent, some insignificant, but all demanding. There are cries for attention that must be answered, for, in most cases, there is no one else to hear. It is from this desk that the pastor goes forth sometimes confident, sometimes fearful, often weary, always humbled by the conviction that he goes not alone. It is at this desk, when the pastor finds a few moments to be alone with his thoughts and God's holy Word, that a sermon is born. This is as it should be, for it is here in a unique way that the world and the Word meet, a world of hungry people and a life-giving Word.

To know the world is not enough. To know the Word is not enough. Both must be known, for preaching that is to meet the challenge of this modern world must be "bifocal." [1] It must be the confrontation of the living God with living people through the living Word. We cannot, we must not, let go of either. We must struggle and fight at this meeting point of world and Word until we are blessed — blessed by divine guidance, insight, and the perseverance to labor for the Lord. It is then, and only then, that we can rise from our desks and go to our pulpits as persons who have seen a vision that must be shared, as persons who have received a message that must be told. And God pity us if this message is not both relevant and eternal, for the age in which we live needs to hear a word from God, not from us — a transcendent Word that brings hope into our despair, light into our darkness, and life into the midst of our death.

The Sermon

As we walk from the desk to the pulpit we take with us a sermon. Recently the sermon has experienced a serious attack that has challenged its very existence. Experts in the field of communication have maintained that there are far more effective means of communicating the gospel than by the traditional speaker standing in a pulpit and preaching a sermon to a silent congregation. Dialogue, multi-media, and a striking array of experimental methods have been suggested and tried. But the tide seems to be changing. Professors of preaching attest to a renewed interest in their subject and enlarged enrollment in their classes. Increasingly, congregations report that they are bored with novelty and simply want to hear a good sermon.

There are reasons for the resurgence of the traditional pulpit-delivered sermon. To begin with, people who hold certain beliefs need to be reminded of the ideas and events which were important to the formation and establishment of their beliefs. They need to have their convictions reinforced. They need someone to reassure them that their beliefs are sound.

The gospel which forms the basis of the Christian faith is a story. Stories need to be told and retold if they are to live. A good story is not something you hear once and know like a fact. A good story is something you want to hear again and agian.

The Christian faith is based on a book. The great themes of the Bible need to be identified and difficult passages need interpretation. And there is always the need for practical application of the biblical message to the current lives of the people of faith. It is true that these ends can be accomplished by means other than the traditional pulpit sermon, but for two thousand years the pulpit with its sermon has been the voice of God to his people.

People need to have their feelings, fears, desires, and opinions verbalized. A skilled speaker can do this. Most of us have experienced listening to a speaker and then saying to ourselves, "That is what I have been thinking for a long time, but I have never been able to put it into words." The sermon puts into words the faith *of* the people as well as expressing the faith *to* the people.

The gospel is not a product resulting from dialogue or discussion. It is something given by tradition. It is not the opinion of the majority or the speculation of a brilliant few. It is a divine revelation that needs a voice to express itself to the people. The gospel needs a spokesperson — an informed, trained, and prepared spokesperson. The gospel is not our story, it is a story for us. The purity of that story must be protected. The pulpit can be a symbol assuring the listener that the person who assumes to speak from this position of leadership is not self-appointed to the task. Rather, he has been trained and tested and is therefore qualified to speak the truth of God's Word, rather than expressing his own opinions and ideas.

True, the system does not always work. There are ministers, preaching boring sermons, who ignore either the truth of the gospel or the needs of the people, or both. But that does not prove the method wrong or out-dated. Preaching should be evaluated not on the basis of its poor examples alone. The fact remains that a well-informed, soundly-educated preacher, who is dedicated to the gospel and has developed his public speaking skills, and is inspired by the Spirit, is still the most direct, precise, reliable and effective means of proclaiming the gospel of Jesus Christ.

The Sermon Defined

It is important to come to a common understanding of what we mean by the word "sermon." Not all preaching involves the delivery of a sermon. A person may stand up and preach on any topic. It is also possible to give a religious address or talk in the pulpit and still not fulfill the requirements of a sermon.

Brilioth, in his book *A Brief History of Preaching*,[2] establishes three basic marks of the sermon: (1) A sermon takes place in a setting of divine worship. (2) A sermon is the development of a text. (3) A sermon is prophetic in that it relates the Word of God to the contemporary situation.

This definition of a sermon is based on Luke 4:14-21, where our Lord comes to Nazareth, enters a synagogue on the Sabbath, and in the process of the service of worship stands up and reads from the Book of Isaiah and then proclaims, "Today this scripture has been fulfilled in your hearing." In this incident all the requirements of a sermon are present: worship, development of a text, and contemporary application.

Such a limited definition of the sermon does not mean that religious address and topical talks on religion have no place in the pulpit. This is simply to make clear that not everything that happens in the pulpit is a sermon. A sermon has an integrity of its own. It is a unique type of public address. If it is to be adequately studied, it needs to be carefully defined.

Text

The first actual step of preparation is the selection of a text. By text we do not necessarily mean one single verse or line of Scripture. One of the calamities of modern preaching is the plague of the small text. Today people do not know the Bible. They are familiar with its cover. They are convinced that every home should have one in case of an emergency, such as a visit from the pastor, but they are not reading it. This biblical illiteracy is in many cases increased by pastors who limit their sermons to small isolated texts each Sunday morning and hammer away at their content. In the mind of the average church attender, the Bible is rapidly becoming a religious scrapbook, a collection of unrelated spiritual and moral sayings, a crazy-quilt of ideas without design or pattern. We have lost the sense of the Bible as the great dramatic pageant of a living God unfolding himself and tearing open his heart upon a cross in a great cosmic struggle to save and redeem humanity, and bring us into eternal fellowship. Therefore, the text must be not a single verse or passage of Scripture withdrawn for special consideration, but a point of focus within the totality of revelation by which we can be brought to a greater understanding of the whole.

Those who are members of a liturgical church have their work already outlined for them in the stated propers of the Church Year. There is a growing awareness and appreciation that these historic passages reveal in an organized fashion the unfolding drama of salvation. If the Church Year is observed, the entire propers for the day should be read and a theme for the day established. This theme will be a comprehensive sentence which states in a clear way what the propers are saying. After stating the theme for the day, select that part of the propers which will serve as the focal point for developing a sermon. If the Gospel is selected, the text may consist of the entire Gospel passage or any desired verse or series of verses within it.

The Eight Steps

Once the text is selected, we are ready to undertake the eight-step process of sermon creation. Each step is important but not absolutely necessary in each case. The creation of a sermon is an elusive experience. It does not always happen in the same way, and it cannot be reduced to a mechanical methodology. Method must always be kept flexible and adjustable to particular happenings.

Inspiration plays a vital role in all creative work. This is particularly true of the sermon. In sermon creation inspiration is that moment when a "spark" occurs and the idea of the sermon suddenly hits you. This may happen anywhere along the line of the suggested process. When it does, you should respond. Drop everything you are doing and follow its leadings.

The eight-step process of sermon creation that we will consider includes Exploration and Research, Confusion, Incubation, Speculation, Reduction, Decision, Condensation and Analysis, and Elaboration. If at any point in these eight steps a "spark" occurs, stop and follow it. It may happen during the first step while you are researching the text. You come across a statement and are convinced that this is the sermon idea you are going to have to preach. Great! Pursue it.

However, if nothing happens in the process of exploration and research, move on to the second step. If no inspiration or spark occurs when you reach step six, which is Decision, then you will have done sufficient work that will hopefully enable you to write the sermon. It will not be as easy as writing under the exciting impulse of inspiration, but some sermons simply have to be methodically constructed. Because of this, we present this eightfold process and utter the personal hope that it will not always have to be followed all the way through.

Step 1 — Exploration and Research

Exploration and research is a study of the chosen passage to establish what the author meant when he wrote it. This will require a knowledge of the background, setting, authorship, and historical circumstances that surrounded the writing. It will involve reading the text in the original language. If this is not possible, then read and compare various translations of the passage. Commentaries should be carefully examined and elaborate notes taken. Underline important words and note new insights.

If you do not know the meaning of a word, take the time to look it up in a theological or biblical dictionary. Definitions often spark sermon ideas. If you have forgotten the full implications of such words as "Spirit" or "faith," turn to a good theological word study and review how the term has been used in the Bible and in theological works.

Then turn to the books written by theologians and biblical scholars that you have in your library. Check references to your text in the index. Examine the context in which your text is used. The spark that ignites the sermon often flashes here. Commentaries approach the passage from an abstract orientation. But when your text appears in the process of developing a theological thought, you see not only its meaning but its use in a particular application. As the author uses the text to explain or define an idea, the text takes on a life and a vitality that is most suggestive for sermon ideas.

Theological journals are helpful in giving you the most current and up-to-date work being done on particular texts and theological thought.

Other Sermons

The question of whether other sermons written on your text should be considered a part of research is a difficult one. The immediate answer is that it all depends on the "other sermons." Many sermons reflect sound and thorough research of a text and penetrating insights into its meaning that can be gathered from no other source. It would be foolish to ignore them.

The danger is that, since these insights and interpretations appear in sermonic form, there is the temptation to copy the sermon idea as your own. Even more damaging is what such sermons do to your own creative process. A sermon can be so attractive that you are captivated by it and can be satisfied with no other approach to the text. You are caught and simply must end up preaching someone else's sermon.

This is not altogether bad. I would rather hear a sermon based on a good sermon, than hear a bad sermon based on nothing but the stumbling efforts of a person who had no idea what a text really meant. I have heard a sermon preached and then on the way home turned on the radio to hear Theodore Parker Ferris deliver one of his masterful sermons on the same text and have thought to myself that the people in the church I had attended would have been better off if their preacher had read Ferris' sermon from the pulpit that morning instead of preaching his own.

The tragedy is that we are caught in the trap of a culture that places total value on individualism. As a result, the pulpit and the sermon are considered as private creations of a professional. The sermon becomes a literary product and therefore the exclusive property of a single preacher. But the truth is, no preacher ever writes a sermon that is totally his own creation, made up exclusively of his own ideas and illustrative materials. Every preacher, even the greatest, stands in the pulpit indebted to many for the final sermon he preaches.

If preachers were not so concerned with self-image, the profession of preaching could become a brotherhood of those dedicated to proclaiming the gospel as effectively and forcefully as possible to all people. When a sermon writer came across an idea, an interpretation, an illustration of merit, he would immediately want to share it with all faced with preaching on this same text. Preaching would be a much more vital force in the lives of people if only we as preachers were not so concerned that this is my insight or yours. It should only concern us that here is an insight or illustration that can be used to make the proclamation of the gospel more powerful and clearer. Because of this it belongs to everybody who can use it.

Certainly Matthew, Mark, and Luke did not hesitate lifting portions of each other's material as they were constructing their Gospels. They were concerned with the clarity and the communication of the gospel and not with their personal reputations as preachers, to the end that they might be called to more pretentious pulpits with the accompanying higher salaries.

I realize that this hope that preaching could be a co-operative effort of a "pastorhood" is at present unrealistic. Congregations would have to be trained to expect not my sermon on Sunday morning, but the expression of the minds of many proclaimers. But just think what would happen to the quality of preaching if this were the case.

True, many lazy preachers would have it made coasting through their ministries on the hard work of others. The truth is that, in some cases, this would not be much different, except that it would make a common practice more honest. But think what it would do for the people in the pew. They would be enriched and blessed by the best that human minds could create under the inspiration of the Spirit and the power of the living Word.

But back to the question of using other sermons as part of research. If you are easily influenced and have difficulty with creative thought, then hold off reading other sermons until you have a firm hold on your own sermon.

On the other hand, if you feel as I do, that it is the gospel that is important and not our personal reputation as an interpreter of it, then use any source that will help you write a better sermon. However, be honest when you accept help from other sermon writers. Of course, never copy the wording of an entire sermon or even of an entire paragraph. Put borrowed ideas in your own words. Otherwise, you will destroy any creative qualities you might have. And your listeners will certainly recognize that what you say sounds artificial and unnatural. If you use a great deal of another person's work, acknowledge your indebtedness in the bulletin or during the announcement period. Direct acknowledgement within the sermon itself should be avoided as it slows down the flow of the sermon and gives an academic tone that is generally detrimental to the conversational style of the sermon.

It is also important when we use ideas and insights from other sermons, that we should not lift the content from those sermons to ours without anything happening in between. Take the idea and mull it over in your mind. Let it percolate in your own personality. Don't take it for your own. Make it your own. Like an adopted child, let it live with you until you deserve the right to use it as your own. And if it succeeds and you get unusually favorable response from using the idea, don't hesitate to share the compliment with the source. Admit that you are indebted to another for seeing this insight into the text.

And take time to educate your people. Let them in on the process whereby you create your sermons. Help them understand that the important thing is not your own personal creative skills or intellectual insights, but that the sermon is a product of many different sources which have all made a vital contribution to its creation. Let them understand that the gospel has spoken to many different people in many different ways and the more we can learn about the full meaning of the gospel through the insights of others the better.

Research as Background

It is important, when we have finished the research, that we should not feel that every insight discovered needs to find expression in the sermon. This is a temptation, but research should be viewed as building a general knowledge of a passage for future use as well as providing ideas for immediate use. Research provides a background for the content of the sermon and gives the speaker a sense of security that what is said in the sermon is supported by sound evidence. The listener is sensitive to the difference between speakers who speak selectively from a solid knowledge of the subject, and those who squeeze their brain like a sponge to force out the last drop of information they possess on a given subject.

Research is not easy, but one thing is certain. Sermon ideas will never come easy without it, and preaching will never become a joy until you are willing to accept the demanding discipline of sound research.

Relate to the Total Gospel

A text should never be considered apart from its context. This is an essential element of researching a text. But it is also important that a text be related to the total gospel of God's redemptive action. The Bible is not a verbatim record of history. It is a witness of faith. The author of a particular book selected certain events to substantiate and enforce a definite experience which he desired to communicate. The intent of the writer is not first to communicate knowledge, but to create faith in the listener. The resurrected Christ confronted the Apostles, changed and transformed their lives. They were new people, redeemed and forgiven, who had discovered a new and cosmic dimension of human existence. The New Testament was written to bring together the important circumstances which led up to and flowed from this crucial turning point of personal and cosmic history — the Crucifixion and Resurrection. Christ did not appear suddenly on the scene of history. He came as the fulfillment of a promise. But when he came he was greater than the promise. He was born out of the past with the redemptive task of transforming the present and fulfilling the future, which he did in a unique and unexpected way. Therefore, to understand the full meaning of any text, the passage must be viewed in the light of the uniqueness of the Christ event and particularly through the events of the cross and the open tomb. The text should also be examined in the light of the Old Testament prophecy and promise. Ask such questions as: "How is this passage related to the Incarnation, the fall, the Ascension?" "How does the reality of human sin affect this passage?" "Does the experience of Pentecost change the basic direction and thrust of this passage?"

We must not ignore the fact that we stand on this side of the cross and are listening to words that were spoken by our Lord before he went to the cross. Christ made many demands when he taught us the will of God, his Father. And he went to the cross precisely because we could not measure up to those demands to fulfill God's will. To take a passage from the New Testament and preach it as if Christ never went to the cross — that his death and resurrection changed nothing — is to distort the true meaning of the text today. When a demand made before the cross is seen through the event of the cross, that demand becomes a gift, because Christ and the Holy Spirit enable us to do what, before the cross, we could never do.

To examine the text in its original setting is necessary, but not sufficient for understanding its full meaning for today. The text is a living Word and therefore needs to be held up and examined in the light of the total revelation of the gospel. My students find that this process of relating the text to the total gospel is often the most fruitful activity of their sermon preparation. The sermon spark often ignites at this exciting point.

Here, as in all research, careful notes should be taken. Remember there is no moment of inspiration more powerful than the moment an idea is born in your mind.

The richness of good preaching is the capacity to capture the relatedness of events within Holy Scripture and to take a text and see how it relates to God's comprehensive plan of transforming all creation to the final state of perfection when the kingdoms of this world will become the kingdom of our God.

Step Two — Confusion

The second step is confusion and frustration. This is not something that we purposely do in the sermon process, but it is something we experience without seeking it. We should recognize and accept confusion and frustration as an expected part of the process.

Up to this point many notes have been taken. Many ideas have been recorded and support material noted. And it now seems like so much wasted effort because nothing has happened. No spark has occurred and you seem as far away from a sermon as you were when you began the process. But do not be discouraged; this is a vital step in the total creative process.

A student told me about visiting his grandparents during his vacation. One morning his grandmother asked him to mow the lawn. He agreed that he would, but one thing after another came up and occupied his time. His grandmother reminded him again and again that the lawn needed to be cut. And he would answer her that he would do it right after the ball game on TV, or after he called Harry on the phone. When she had reminded him several more times, he finally dropped what he was doing and mowed the lawn.

That night he heard his grandfather say to his grandmother, "How do you have the patience to tell the blockhead twenty times to mow the lawn?" His grandmother answered, "Well, if I would have told him only nineteen times all my effort would have been in vain."

That is the way it is with research. You have to go after a text again and again. Look at it from many different perspectives. Search out every possible idea. The sheer mass of the material will be confusing and frustrating. It will lay on your desk as a mountain of notes meaning nothing. But it is not wasted effort. Somewhere within that confusion are the potential ingredients for a sermon. You must now discover the formula, the order, the form, the recipe that will move like a magnet over the material and pull things together. Then you will see a sermon beginning to take shape, as sure as Grandmother's efforts finally were rewarded with a mowed lawn.

Step Three — Incubation

The third step is incubation. You let your research material rest. The human mind is an interesting and surprising phenomenon. It works when we are unaware of it and when we are not directly giving it orders.

Sleep, for example, is often considered an important part of the creative act and the decision-making process. We say, "Let me sleep on it." And that often helps. Ideas have a way of developing when you let them alone and permit them to take the form they wish to follow.

When we are concentrating on one idea, we prohibit it from making contact with other ideas we already hold. Often, in this interplay among ideas, new ideas are born. Like an artist, we need to step back from our work and let forms and colors blend into each other to form a total composition or pattern.

At this point in the process we need to stop working on the sermon and turn our attention to something else so that the mind is free to get it all together. This we call incubation. And that is why it is so important that we start our sermon preparation early in the week so that there will be plenty of time for the incubation process.

A sermon completed too early in the week often cools off to the point that it possesses none of the creative excitement of its birth when you carry it into the pulpit.

And it is also true that, as far as creative sermon formation is concerned, the preacher who finishes the sermon on Monday for the following Sunday is just as wrong as the person who waits until Saturday night to begin the sermon. Both are rushing the creative process, when creation under normal circumstances takes time.

I had a friend who was a noted water color artist. I have watched him paint and I felt that he was receiving phenomenal prices for work that seemed so simple and easy. He would sit down and whip off a water color in about thirty minutes. What I learned later caused me to radically change my opinion. I discovered that when he decided on a subject matter for his painting, he would go back again and again to the scene. He would make sketch after sketch of it. He would experiment with color. He would let the subject matter relate to him in many different ways. He would view it in the light of his changing moods, so that when the time came for him to touch the final work he would have weeks of relating to his subject matter before he ever put it into its finished form.

So with the creative sermon. It is not something we sit down and hammer out because we need a sermon next Sunday morning. It is, rather, born out of a process of relating to a text and its meaning. And this process includes time for incubation, time for the sermon to find its own inherent form and shape and not be forced into an outline remembered from a beginning textbook on homiletics.

Step Four — Speculation

The fourth step in the creative process, Speculation, is similar to incubation. It, too, includes setting the mind free. But it is different, in that it involves a carefully observed freedom.

Speculation is asking the question, "Now that I have some idea of what God desires to say through this text, what particular message does the text have for the people who will hear this sermon?" Speculation is the fun part of the creative process for me. Certainly it is the most exciting.

Speculation is the bridge between God and his people, between Word and world, between the total gospel and that particular apsect of the gospel that is directed to this particular people in this place and this time.

We need to know our people, their feelings, their desires, their needs, as well as the Bible and its witness. We also need to know the world and the contemporary events which are influencing and shaping the lives of our people. For here in this sermon God brings together his Word and his people.

The sermon, as we have pointed out, is what happens when the Word and the world are brought together. When the right contact is made, a spark ignites, flashes, and bursts into light, and a sermon is born. As we have seen, this is not always an immediate or automatic happening like the touching of two charged wires. We have to first find the right things to bring together, and that is why speculation is a vital part of the creative sermon process.

Sometimes this part of the process is called "brainstorming the text." "Brainstorming" is the random searching out of all the implications of a given idea. Brainstorming requires freedom and movement of thought. The mind is set free and the imagination is released to go in any and all directions.

If the office or study is too noisy, find a place where there are no distractions, perhaps take a walk, or go into the empty church where you preach. Mull over what you have learned about the text. Let your mind wander from one idea to another. As you do, search for the idea that will point up the significance of the text as a whole. Look for an idea that will take the shapeless mass of information you have gathered and bring it all to a point of convergence. Don't neglect any implications of an idea. Follow every lead like a detective attempting to solve a crime. *But, most important of all, keep your people in mind.*

Visualize people before you. See where they are, what they need, what they long and hope for. Examine your own needs and hopes. Then literally play with the various meanings of the text and your people's needs. Move back and forth from people to text, from one idea to another, from idea to need.

If a spark occurs, stop. Write your thoughts on paper as fast as you can. Let thoughts flow forth on the page. At this point don't worry about correct wording or sound textual relatedness. Just write. When you have finished, then you can go back and correct the wording and tighten up the textual soundness.

When you have finished all the writing you can, while under this spark of inspiration, you may have the rough draft of the sermon you will eventually carry into the pulpit. In most cases, however, you will have only sections of a sermon which will demand much more work cutting and pruning and, in general, tightening up material into a structured vehicle for preaching.

It may be necessary to go back over the written material to discover the theme that dominates what you have written. Also look for the structure that holds the writing together. Then rewrite to get the material to better fit the structure. Some sermon writers work first from an outline and then carefully follow it as they write the sermon. Others simply write and then go back and draw the outline out of what they have written. This means that the sermon will have to be adjusted to fit the outline that comes from it.

Helmut Thielicke told the students at our seminary that he generally does not research a text and then write his sermon. He first brainstorms the text. Then when the sermon is finished, he does the research to test the validity of what he has written. He pointed out that creative work in his case was best accomplished when his mind was fresh. If he did the research first, he was tired when it came to the point of writing the sermon.

For the beginning student of preaching, we should point out that this method is an option only when the sermon writer has a solid knowledge of the Scripture before he looks at a text and begins the brainstorming process. This does, however, show the flexibility of the creative process and that we can depend on precise methods only as guides to sermon writing. Ultimately, every writer must discover the method best suited to one's own creative process.

Let us assume that you have gone through the Speculation step of preparation. You have brainstormed the text, gathered a lot of good insights, ideas, even illustrations, but you still are not ready to construct the sermon. Then move to step five, Reduction.

Step Five — Reduction

Reduction is the beginning of organization. Take the notes you have gathered from the previous four steps and review them.

As you read a page or a paragraph, circle key words that represent the ideas it contains. This will make your notes more workable and easier to handle. Then, if you need to review the material again, all you will have to be concerned with are selected words on a page rather than the total number of words. It will also help to identify important ideas.

Look for ideas that stand out and appear more often than others. For example:

(1) An idea might be important because many sources mention the same idea.

(2) An idea might be important because it is new, different, or unique.

(3) An idea might be important because it answers an issue, a problem, a situation that your brainstorming of

the text has indicated is reflected in the lives of your people.

(4) An idea might be important simply because you like it and it appeals to you.

Now select the important ideas and review them. Which seems to be the most important and the most attractive? Write these selected ideas down on a separate piece of paper. One of them is going to be the idea that will form the basis of your sermon. You are now ready for step number six, Decision.

Step Six — Decision

If you have gone this far in the process without a spark occurring that ignites the sermon, this is a crucial step. And it is the most difficult.

You must make a decision. You must select one idea and commit yourself to it. You must take one idea and run with it. How do you make this decision? There is no better advice than simply, "Do it." The ideas before you are the result of a process which provides what is necessary for a sermon. Each idea can be developed into a sermon on the basis of the work you have done up to this point. Therefore, choose one. You will never know if it is the right one until you develop it. If you have four ideas before you, reduce them to three and then to two and finally to one. You have the chosen idea.

The importance of taking this step quickly cannot be stressed too strongly. More time and energy are wasted at this point in sermon preparation than at any other. Make the decision, select the idea, and follow through on the next two steps of the process. Write the sermon. If you then discover that you made a wrong decision and the resulting sermon is impossible to preach, go back and select another idea and develop it. This will be a discouraging experience, but better to write another sermon than to face the pulpit with a sermon that you know is just not right. The discarded sermon will not be a waste of time, for you will have definitely eliminated one idea from your list of possible sermon ideas.

Step Seven — Condensation and Analysis

The seventh step is condensation and analysis. Now you examine the idea you have selected as the basis of the sermon and identify the subject of the idea. What is the idea talking about? Tie this down to a single word, such as love or fear or faith. The key word is usually a noun and is comprehensive in scope. It is what the sermon is going to "talk" about.

Next, analyze the idea to establish in a single sentence what the chosen idea says about the general subject, the key word. For example, the general subject or key word might be love. And what the idea says about it is, "In the New Testament the important thing is not that we are to love but that we are loved, because before you can love you must first be loved." Now this idea has a form. Attempt to find this form. You do this by placing the idea over against the text from which the idea comes. In this case, the idea came from a research of Mark 2:1-12, where the paralytic is lowered through the roof to the feet of Jesus. The first thing that Jesus says to the man is, "Your sins are forgiven." In modern idiom this means, "God is not angry with you" or "God loves you." Jesus begins the process of transforming and changing this man's life by announcing to him that he is loved. It does no good to tell a person to walk until you have placed him on his feet. You must enable him to stand up. The knowledge that we are loved does just that.

Then place the idea over against where you think your listeners are. Is this a new thought for them? Will the listeners have to readjust their views of love? Do they think that the most important thing is simply that we are to love others? If so, where did they get this idea? Did they learn it in church, or from the books they read, or the movies they have seen, or the songs they have sung?

Or does this idea answer a problem that the people have? Is the problem that they try to follow the commandment to love others but find that they cannot? Then here is the place to start. Or do the listeners already accept this idea that you must first be loved because they have learned it by experience in their own lives?

The form which an idea possesses is made up primarily of sequence and emphasis. Sequence simply means that we think about one thing at a time. Why we think about one thing before another is what gives form to any idea. We need to recognize the sequence of thought within an idea.

Emphasis gives different values to certain words or thought-units that make up an idea. When we speak an idea, we break it up into words and phrases. One is more important than another. In the example, the emphasis depends on contrast, the contrast between "being loved" and "loving." And the whole idea depends on sequence that we must first be loved before we can love.

Establishing the sequence and the emphasis of the thought-units or phrases that make up an idea suggests the form of the idea. And the form of the idea determines or at least suggests the structure the sermon will follow.

In many cases the structure of the sermon will be suggested by the text itself. The text, like a sermon idea, possesses sequence and emphasis. Things happen in a certain order and some things are more important than others. The research done on the text should help establish the emphasis points of the text and give a possible structure to follow in the sermon.

The important thing is not so much the structure selected for the sermon but that the speaker makes the structure clear. As you analyze an idea or a text you may see in it a different sequence or emphasis, different points from what I would when faced with the same idea or text. The important thing is that when you stand in the pulpit and present the sermon, the structure is clear and can be easily followed by the listeners. We will deal with this in the chapters which follow.

Step Eight — Elaboration

Elaboration is permitting the idea to develop into the fully structured sermon. This is a massive step and rather than treating it as a section of this chapter, it will be dealt with in the next chapter.

3

The Structure of the Sermon

The sermon is a unique type of pulpit address, but it is a speech and should conform to the structure basic to a good speech.

The Flight of a Bumble Bee

A good speech is like a bumble bee. It possesses five basic parts, each one playing a vital function in the total process of the flight of a bumble bee: a head, a body, a stinger, legs, and wings. They enable both the bumble bee and the speech to get off the ground and do their work.

Every living bee must have a body, and the body of a living speech is that bulk of material which forms the speech's content. It is the message of the speech.

The head of the bumble bee possesses eyes that enable the bee to know where he is, and where he is going. The head of the speech is the introduction. It, too, has two points of vision. One is on the listener, the other is on content. The introduction begins where the people are and informs them where they are going as they listen to the speech that follows.

The stinger is the business end of the bumble bee. The conclusion is the stinger of the speech and is the last opportunity the speaker has to drive home the point of the speech effectively.

Legs support the bumble bee. So a speech needs its supports, evidence and examples that validate the truth and credibility of what is being said.

Then there are the wings. They lift the bee and give him movement. So the illustrations are the wings of the speech. They create interest, give color, and make the content clear and easy to remember.

Now let us look at the basic parts of a good bumble bee and a good speech and see how they specifically apply to the sermon.

Introduction
The Head of the Sermon

The head of a bee is connected to the body, but at the same time different from it. It is unique with distinct and separate functions from the rest of the body.

So with the introduction. It is not the first point of the body of the sermon. It is separate from the body of the sermon. It is related to the body but has its own integrity based on the distinct functions it is to perform:

1. The introduction should first of all acknowledge the listener. A sermon is not an essay on a topic. It is not a term paper on a given subject. It is not a Sunday School lecture on a lesson. The sermon is a personal message from God to his people. Therefore, the first sentence of the sermon should be addressed to the listener.

For example, a Lenten sermon about Judas began, "Judas is remembered not as a disciple but as a traitor." This would be an adequate beginning sentence for an essay or a lecture about Judas, but not for a sermon. It focuses the attention on the subject matter when it should be on the listener. The suggested change:

It is doubtful that any of you men here this evening have the given name of Judas. We frequently name our children John, James, and Peter. But no one would consider naming their bouncing baby boy Judas. For Judas is remembered not as a disciple but as a traitor.

Now the introduction speaks directly and personally to the listeners. It acknowledges the listeners and hopefully sets the tone for the sermon which is to follow.

2. The introduction should begin where the people are. In most cases this is not where they should be so far as the content of the sermon is concerned, but we begin where they are and then take them to where they should be. So, we begin with a need, a concern, an interest of the listeners. However, it is not always easy to know where the listeners are, for people are not alike. But if we are sensitive to the congregation, maintain a close personal contact with them and their daily lives, we will be able to recognize common needs and interests that apply to most of the listeners.

One thing is certain: They are not where the text of the sermon is. They are in the 20th century America. They are not in Jerusalem in the first century. *So the sermon should rarely begin in the setting of the text.*

Remember that we come to the sermon with hours of study and background preparation. The listeners come to the sermon cold. We have the advantage of seeing the connection between the text and life, and therefore we have a pre-established interest in the text. The listeners do not have the capacity to read our thoughts, or share our interest in the text, until we have established contact with their minds. We do this by beginning where the people are.

3. The introduction should capture the attention of the listeners. So far as the majority of the congregation is concerned, this will not be too difficult. They have come to church wanting to hear what God has to say to them. Therefore, the introduction should be aimed at the disinterested, those who came to church because they were brought by spouse, parents, or friends. They would prefer being almost anywhere else. Then there are those who came to church out of habit, or sense of duty. For them the sermon is a fifteen or twenty minute interruption in an otherwise smooth-flowing service. They are easy to spot, for they always look at their watches before we begin to preach. Someone has said that for many churchgoers, the sermon is the

"Protestant penitence." It is what the believer must endure to assure God's blessings.

It is to these disinterested that the content of the introduction should be directed. We might get their attention by establishing their good will. This again points up the importance of a friendly attitude when entering the pulpit and beginning the sermon. A simple smile might win them over. Or we might try to arouse their curiosity. Ask a question or pose a problem that would create a sense of expectation of what is to follow. But, most importantly, try to appeal to their interests. We can be fairly certain that their interests are not going to be "religious." Introductions therefore should be marked by life-situation interests. The average person is interested in other people, what happens to them, what they do and how they think. Children have a universal appeal. Current events, sports, entertainment, politics, eating, vacations, and travel all offer built-in interest factors.

We might miss. We might fail to capture the attention of the disinterested, but at least we will have tried and hopefully they will have sensed it.

4. The next function of the introduction is that it should be appropriate to the sermon and really introduce the subject matter which is to follow.

There are many ways to get people's attention. We could step into the pulpit and shoot a gun. That would certainly demand attention, but the sermon could hardly measure up to such an introduction, and a good introduction should never promise anything that the sermon cannot possibly deliver.

Sensational and shocking introductions should also be handled carefully and used sparingly. I once heard a sermon which began, "You are going to Hell on your buts." The preacher got attention and he hurriedly went on to clarify his meaning after seeing the looks on the faces of his startled parishioners. He pointed out that, when faced with service opportunities within the church, we answer, "I would like to do it, but . . ." Such a startling statement fulfilled all the requirements of a good introduction, but many people in the congregation were turned off by it. An introduction should exhibit good taste.

Once when preaching a sermon that involved procrastination, I walked into the pulpit and apologized for having no sermon ready for the worship service that morning. I explained that things had been so hectic in the past week that I simply had no time to prepare a sermon. I sat down. After a short pause which seemed quite long, both to me and the congregation, I returned to the pulpit and pointed out that this is what God experiences again and again as he waits for our responsive use of the grace he has given us. Then I proceeded with the sermon.

Such introductions are effective and unforgettable. And that is the point. They are remembered and can be used effectively only once. You can't fool the congregation twice in a row. The other problem with this sensational type of introduction is what do you do next Sunday? There are just so many tricks that can be used. So the best advice is to use sensational types of introductions sparingly and avoid setting a pattern of expectation in the minds of the congregation for shocking introductions.

5. The introduction should begin at the emotional level of the listeners. The congregation finishes the hymn, settles back to hear the sermon, and suddenly the preacher explodes in the pulpit. He is enthusiastic and pitches his introduction at an emotional level far beyond where his listeners are. It is much like the man who stalled his car on the highway. He flagged down a lady motorist and asked her to give his car a push. He carefully explained that his car had to go about thirty miles per hour before the engine would kick over. The lady agreed. He waited. Nothing happened. Then a horrible thought entered his mind and he looked fearfully into the rear view mirror. His panic was

confirmed, for he saw the lady in her car about two hundred feet down the highway bearing down on him at thirty miles per hour. This is frequently what happens in the pulpit. The congregation is emotionally at a standstill and the preacher jumps into the pulpit and heads his sermon at them going three hundred words per minute.

In the theater this is called "anticipation." The speaker is thinking ahead to what he is going to say rather than concentrating on what he is saying. We anticipate the exciting content that the sermon has in store for the listeners, but the congregation must be brought to share this excitement, not be suddenly struck by it.

The comment is made frequently that a preacher is too emotional in his presentation. The truth is that, in most cases, he was not necessarily too emotional but he failed to bring his listeners up to the same emotional level on which he was operating. The amount of emotion displayed in the pulpit, as well as the amount of excitement, depends on how skillful the speaker is in bringing his listeners up to a level that matches his own emotion, enthusiasm, and excitement.

I have passed by revival meetings and heard the hand-clapping and the foot-stomping and thought to myself, "That's not for me." But I have attended some of these revivals. At first I maintained the dignity of an observer, but as the meeting wore on I found my foot beginning to tap and before long I was clapping along with the rest of them. Strangely enough it seemed natural. I had been carried to the point where I could participate and share the emotional level and therefore not object to it. Emotions and enthusiasm in the pulpit, as in all aspects of the preaching process, need to be a shared experience if they are to be acceptable to the listeners.

6. The introduction should be as brief as possible. It should move the listeners rapidly into the body of the sermon. This will mean careful attention to the choice of

words. If no other part of the sermon is written in manuscript form, the introduction should be. Lack of wordiness at this point is essential.

It is dangerous to establish a rule for such things, but an approximation would be that for a fifteen-seventeen minute sermon, the introduction should not exceed one minute. Since the average person speaks about 120 words a minute, a maximum introduction should consist of no more than 120 words.

7. The last consideration of the function of the introduction is transition. On the bumble bee this would correspond to his neck, that which connects the head to the body. We have stressed that the introduction possesses an integrity of its own, but a vital part of that integrity is its relationship to the body of the sermon.

This point of contact between introduction and the body of the sermon in most cases involves the text. We have stated that the introduction begins where the people are, in the full realization that they are not where they should be, and then proceeds to take them where they should be. Since the sermon is based on a text, this is where the listener must eventually be brought. Thus, the last sentence of the introduction should lead naturally and logically to that portion of the text on which the sermon will be developed.

In summary, the function of the introduction is to:

(1) acknowledge the listeners

(2) begin where the listeners are and take them to where they should be

(3) capture the attention of the disinterested

(4) introduce the listeners to the content of the sermon which follows

(5) establish a compatible emotional level with the listeners

(6) move as quickly and smoothly into the body of the sermon as possible, and

(7) form a transition to the text and sermon content.

Conclusion
The Stinger of the Sermon

The stinger is the business end of the bee. The stinger in the sermon is the conclusion, the last contact made with the listeners. It is here that the point of the sermon should be seen most clearly and felt most sharply, so that it can be carried back into the daily lives of the listeners.

The conclusion, however, has often been the most neglected part of the sermon. In many cases, there is no conclusion — the sermon simply ends. Like the introduction, it is not part of the body of the sermon. The conclusion possesses its own integrity and is designed for specific functions:

1. The conclusion should give a sense of completeness to the sermon. Since it is not a part of the body, it should introduce no new ideas, but should summarize and review what has been said.

Many sermon writers confuse conclusion with climax. The climax of the sermon is that point toward which everything in the sermon should move. It is the point that really accomplishes and presents the purpose of the sermon. Everything should move toward and flow from the climax. The climax may occur at any point in the total development. It is conceivable that the climax could be placed at the very beginning of the body of the sermon, and the whole sermon would therefore flow naturally, logically, and inevitably from it. Generally the climax is placed past the middle of the sermon's development and in most cases near the end. If the climax is at the very end of the body of the sermon, there is still a need for a conclusion. The function of the climax is to make the point of the sermon. The function of the conclusion is not to make the point, but to drive home the point that has already been made.

2. This leads us to the second requirement of the conclusion: It should enforce the main thrust of the

sermon. This is generally done by appealing to the will and the emotions of the listeners rather than to their reasoning. The function of the conclusion is to move the listeners to accept what has been said in the body of the sermon, and act upon it.

The conclusion is often in the form of a challenge or a promise. It sometimes extends an invitation or gives a benediction in the form of a word of hope that the message of the sermon may bear fruit in the listeners' lives.

The story is a common technique for concluding a sermon. It should be one which summarizes what has been said in the sermon. Stories are easily remembered. So if the message of the sermon is embodied in the form of a story, it enables the listeners to remember the message by remembering the story.

3. The conclusion of a sermon should, in most cases, be positive. It should seldom be conditional, except when the sermon has presented its theme so completely and powerfully that only one conclusion can be reached.

One popular way to end a sermon is with a question. But this generally gives the impression that a case has been presented to a jury and now they are to arrive at a verdict. Such an approach to preaching seems contrary to the nature of the gospel, which is not so much an appeal for us to accept Christ, but the good news that Christ has chosen and accepted us.

For example, when a sermon ends on the note, "If you believe, if you surrender, if you have faith . . .", the whole results of the sermon depend exclusively upon the listener. If we acknowledge the power of the Word and the work and the activity of the Holy Spirit in the sermon process, then it would seem it would be better to end on the note of promise rather than condition. Instead of saying "If you believe," say "When you believe, such and such will happen." This takes into consideration both the efficacious power of the Word and the hope that the Holy Spirit will work in the lives of the listeners because of the sermon. A gospel sermon should end on the note of the promise of God rather than on the verdict of humanity. The conclusion is still open for people to reject the Word and resist the Spirit, but the positive ending offers every opportunity to permit the Word and the Spirit to work.

4. The first few sentences of the conclusion should establish in the listeners' minds the suggestion that the sermon is moving to the end. This is frequently accomplished by referring back to the subject matter, the wording, or the images established in the introduction.

For example: the Lenten sermon about Judas began with the idea that few if any men in the congregation have been given the name of Judas and we would not think of naming our children Judas. The sermon which followed presented the idea that Judas should not be condemned so much as pitied, for he tried so desperately to control the destiny of his own life. He tragically attempted to rectify his mistakes by hanging himself. The conclusion would then begin:

> *Therefore, even though we still will not name our boy babies Judas, perhaps we will be more sympathetic to the role of Judas in the Christ event, for he stands as a warning to all of us who attempt to take the destiny of our lives into our own hands.*

The reference in the first sentence of the conclusion to the idea expressed in the introduction about naming our children after Judas gives a clue to the listeners that we are coming to the end of the sermon. It gives a sense of completeness to the sermon as we have come back to where we began. Yet we are far different people for having experienced the development of the sermon.

In summary, then, the conclusion should complete the sermon. It should add no new ideas, but summarize and review for the listener what has been said. But most of all, the conclusion should enforce the point of the sermon and drive it home like a stinger. This means that it should end on a definite and positive note of promise.

False Conclusions

One more thing needs to be said concerning the conclusion. The greatest danger concerning the concluding part of the sermon is false conclusions — saying something that gives the impression we have reached the conclusion when we have not. This is generally the result of poor planning, uncertain thinking, and careless choice of words. Like the introduction, the conclusion should be written out in full. I spend more time on the exact wording of the introduction and the conclusion than I do on any other part of the sermon.

I frequently demonstrate the importance of the introduction and conclusion to my first-year students by bringing two upper-class students into class to give short speeches. The one student has a terrific introduction and a dynamic conclusion, but says little or nothing in the body of his talk. The other speaker has a sloppy introduction and a dull and messy conclusion, but the body of the talk possesses some very solid material of worth. Then I ask the juniors to evaluate the speakers. In almost every case, they rate first the student with the great introduction and conclusion but nothing much to say. This has been a strong suggestion to me to respect the integrity and importance of both the introduction and the conclusion.

Support Material
The Legs of the Sermon

The legs give the bee his support. So the content of the sermon needs material to support the points made. As we have said, a gospel sermon is not a legal case argued before a jury. The Word of God needs no defense and does not depend on proof. The Word, however, does need definition, explanation, and application. This is the function of support material.

As the sermon develops, there is the constant need to relate what is being said to the text. The preacher knows the connection and sees the relationship between content and text, but the listener may not. Therefore, this relationship needs to be pointed out.

Since the sermon is a dialogue of thought between speaker and listeners, when the listeners are expected to think back or relate content to text, they must have time to do it. Therefore, the speaker should verbalize the action so that speaker and listeners stay together in the thought process. Otherwise, the speaker moves ahead to a new idea when the listeners are still trying to see the relationship of the last thought to the text or to a previous idea.

1. Definition. One of the most important of all support materials is definition. It establishes the meaning of a word. But even more, in the speaking situation, it establishes a mutual agreement of what the meaning of the word is. A word may have different meanings for different people. Therefore, the vital thing is that speaker and listener agree as to what a word means. This is best accomplished by examples taken from everyday life.

Consider the word "eschatology." The other evening I was watching TV. It was an exciting mystery story. Near the end of the program the telephone rang. I went to answer it. When the conversation was finished I returned to the TV. The commercial was on. The program was over and I never found out who committed the crime. The story lost its meaning because I had no idea how it turned out in the end. That is the meaning of eschatology. The end determines the meaning and value of all that precedes it. Admittedly, such an example and definition does not exhaust the meaning of eschatology.

It is not a theological dictionary's definition of the term. But it is the meaning I have in mind as I will use the word in the content of the sermon. Therefore, definition as support material is not just defining a word, but establishing a mutual agreement between speaker and listener on how the word will be used in the sermon.

2. *Explanation.* Close to definition is explanation, but it carries with it an added dimension or function. Definition is a mutual agreement between speaker and listener on how a word will be used. Explanation interprets an idea and gives reasons. It answers the questions of "why" and "how." For example, a definition of eschatology is that the end determines the meaning and value of all that goes before it. An explanation of eschatology would attempt to show how and why the end determines the meaning of all that goes before it. It does not simply define a term or idea; it analyzes it, resolves it into its basic elements, separates it into its basic parts so that the term or idea may be better understood.

3. *Application.* In the traditional approach toward sermon preparation, application was the third division of the basic sermon structure, the other two being exegesis and exposition. Application generally followed exegesis and exposition. However, application is better thought of as a form of support running through the entire sermon. When application is treated as a stage in the sermon's development, it appears to be artificial, something that the speaker adds to an idea rather than something spontaneously arising out of the idea itself. We should not give the impression that we are now going to apply the idea to daily life. Rather we should point out how the idea applies itself to the life situation.

Too often, application is an attempt on the part of the speaker to prove the validity of a text. It should be the other way around. It is the validity of the life situation that is established by the text. We do not apply the text to life; rather, we relate life situations to the text.

Proof Texts

Passages from the Bible are frequently used as support material to a point made in the sermon. Because of the interrelatedness of the Bible's content, this would seem to be an effective process. However, because of the biblical illiteracy that presently prevails, proof texting should be used cautiously. Frequently the preacher uses another biblical passage to support the text and that passage is less familiar than the text.

When you move beyond a few simple Bible stories found in the Old Testament and the major events in the life of Christ in the New Testament, most listeners are lost in the Bible. What is needed is for the sermon to stick to its own text and develop that as clearly and completely as possible. In most cases, bringing in other passages from the Bible for support only confuses the issue.

In summary, we support the ideas of the sermon with definition, explanation, and application. In each case, examples from life situations are vital. This brings us to another support of the content of the sermon — the illustration. The illustration, however, does more than support the material of the sermon; it lifts it.

Illustration
The Wings of the Bumble Bee

Wings lift the bumble bee and enable it to move. Illustrations well chosen and delivered not only make a sermon clear and understandable, but intersting and entertaining as well. Illustrations give the sermon lift and movement.

Illustrations come in various artistic sizes and styles. Some are just quick splashes of color, others are snapshots, while still others are detailed paintings.

1. Splashes of colorful writing give sparkle and interest to the sermon. They are fresh use of words,

picturesque phrases, and expressions. For example, one student talking about a famous football player said, "He may not always make the tackle, but he always makes the play."

In this TV-watching age, one student wrote this fresh reference to the fall: "Man has tangled, distorted, and knocked out of focus the creation of which he is a part. And there is no switch he can flick to make it right again."

Here is a paragraph from a sermon by David Redding, a master at the use of fresh and colorful writing.

> One of God's good ideas was to get some light on creation and then to pass out to each person a pair of tiny windows so that everyone could see what he was doing. Who can fathom what a fairy tale it is to wake up in the morning with our own private eyes, two shining jewels to each man, and to see for ourselves the dazzling splendor of day and night? Our eyes "open Sesame" to stars dancing on black velvet, daffodils drifting in a sea of gold, falling petals of snow, the face of a child in prayer. Our other presents may seem small beside our sight. What right have we who see to grumble?1

These phrases like "make the tackle," "flick the switch," "stars dancing on black velvet," "the face of a child at prayer," add interest and color to the sermon. They are words not just to convey meaning but to delight our ear and excite the imagination.

2. Then there are snapshot illustrations, short little examples that create instant pictures in the mind. They do not argue with our minds, but they invite our minds to see something interesting.

In class one day the students were struggling with humanity's role in the process of salvation. Somehow they couldn't get hold of it. Either they gave humanity too little or too much participation in the process. On the way home from class I saw a student raking leaves in his backyard, and then carrying them in huge bags to the street. As the student came around the house, behind him came his three-year-old son. In his tiny fist he had a few leaves. He was helping his father. His contribution amounted to nothing. The job could have been done just as well without his help. But think what it meant to that little fellow to feel he had a part in the process. Here was the perfect illustration of what I was trying to get across to my students. Just a snapshot example from life, but it enabled my class to see what I was trying to say with wordy explanations.

3. Then there are detailed paintings — story illustrations. They possess characters, dialogue, and a plot. One of my students told about his daughter who came home from school with the assignment of making a world globe out of a plastic ball. At the dining room table she cut out all the various continents from a map of the world. But while she was in the kitchen getting the glue, her baby sister climbed up to the dining room table. She ate up Africa, crushed Europe into a wad, and tore Asia in half. When the older sister returned from the kitchen and saw what had happened, she flew into a rage, and shouted, "Stupid blockhead! Look what you've done, you naughty girl." Her baby sister burst into tears of fright. Seeing this reaction, the temper of the older sister cooled and she went over to her baby sister, put her arms around her and said, "Don't cry. You've torn up my world, but I still love you."

Such story illustrations contribute much to a sermon. They not only make a point, but they appeal to our emotions. They need to be carefully written to avoid wordiness and needless details. The exact point that you want to make with the story needs to be identified. Then you include just enough detail to put that point across effectively. For example, in the above story, the point is what the older sister says: "You've torn up my world, but I still love you." Now you include just enough of the total account of what happened to make that single sentence uttered by the older sister meaningful. This is different from writing a short story for a magazine where the composition of the story is the important thing. You are using the story to make a point, to illustrate an idea. You are not just telling a story.

There is no such thing as a good sermon illustration. There is only an illustration in a sermon that makes a point well. Therefore, write your illustrations carefully so that they do not call attention to themselves, but to the point you want to make.

The number of story illustrations used in a sermon should be limited. Too many long stories in one sermon tend to fight each other. The effectiveness of the story illustration is that it enables the listener to remember the point made by remembering the story. But if you give the listeners too many stories to remember, then both the stories and the points will be lost in the confusion of trying to remember everything that was said.

Many times the text determines the need and use of story illustrations. If the text is itself a story, such as a parable or a miracle, then story illustrations are not as necessary as when the text is a statement made by Christ, or a comment by Paul, or a general lesson or teaching from the Bible.

The important thing to remember when considering how a point needs to be illustrated is that stories are not the only type of illustration. In fact, colorful phrases, picturesque statements, fresh wording, short examples, are far more determinative to the well-illustrated sermon than are lengthy stories. Stories are good and impressive in the sermon, but picturesque writing is what makes the total sermon exciting and interesting. A dull sermon can often be saved by a few good story illustrations, but in the long run, writing style can make of the whole sermon an interesting illustration of the meaning of the text.

Purpose of the Illustration

Now to the purpose of the illustration. We have said that the main purpose is to illustrate a point or an idea made in the sermon. Let's expand on that.

1. An illustration is used to clarify an idea. This can be done first of all by creating a picture in the minds of the listeners. For example, the preacher may say, "Similar to your baptism." Or you could create a picture: "Similar to the time when your parents carried you as a baby to the font and water was poured over your head." The second way of conveying the idea doesn't depend on the listeners creating their own image, but the picture is created for them by the speaker. In oral communication where there is no time to think beyond the words of the speaker, this is very important. When we read words, we can pause and think back to an experience such as our baptism. But when we are listening to words being spoken, and we stop to think, the speaker does not stop. When we return to listening to what is being said, the speaker has moved ahead to another idea and we are frequently lost. Therefore, when important words in an idea need reflective thought, create the picture for your listeners. Or, perhaps better said, create the picture with your listeners.

A second way an idea can be clarified is by relating it to something familiar. This is generally in the form of an example, a simile, or a metaphor. A student preaching on the Beatitudes was attempting to clarify meekness. He said, "It is like domesticating a wild animal. All the strength, energy, vitality of the animal is retained, but it is now disciplined and controlled. Meekness is not being a Mr. Milquetoast, but simply being a well-mannered, thoughtful, kind person." This not only clarified what the word meant, but corrected a common misunderstanding of the word.

A third way a word or idea can be clarified is by following it with a more familiar word or phrase. These are referred to as "trailers." For example, the speaker says, "Most of us are frequently guilty of procrastination, putting things off." The little phrase, "putting things off," trails the more complex word and clarifies it. This subtle approach avoids the possible danger of a more obvious definition which sometimes gives the impression that the listener is too dumb to know the meaning of "procrastination." Some words demand full definition, while others need only a "trailer" word or phrase to clarify their meaning.

The fourth way to clarify an idea is with a full story illustration, which we have already dealt with.

2. *Illustrations are also used to enforce an idea.* Here the idea is clear enough but the speaker wants to emphasize its importance. In a sermon that was presenting the idea that we need to know that we are loved, the story was told of Karl Barth, the father of 20th century theology. While Barth was lecturing in this country, a seminary student asked him, "What is the most profound insight that has been revealed to you in your many years of scholarly study of the Scriptures?" Dr. Barth reportedly hesitated for a moment and then leaned over the lecture desk and began to sing," Jesus loves me, this I know, for the Bible tells me so." The contrast between the brilliant theological mind of Barth and the simple words of a child's hymn gave a forceful impact to our need to know that we are loved.

3. *Another purpose of the illustration is to involve the listener.* The listeners might understand an idea and see its value, but do not identify with the idea. An illustration is therefore needed to touch the feelings and emotions of the listeners. Actually the purpose here is to get the listeners to react to the idea. Its purpose is empathy. The idea becomes related to the hearer by an emotional reaction to the illustration.

Winston Churchill told the story of a sailor who dove into the waters of Plymouth Harbor and saved the life of a little boy. Several days later the sailor came across the same little boy and his mother on the streets of

Plymouth. The boy nudged his mother and she stopped. "Are you the man who pulled my little boy out of the water?" she asked. Expecting a word of gratitude the sailor smiled, saluted, and said, "Yes, Ma'am." "Then," snapped back the mother, "where's his cap?" We can all identify with the sailor's feelings. As a listener to the story we literally "feel" the meaning of ingratitude. We become involved to the point of wishing we could have been there to "put that mother straight."

4. *The final purpose of the illustration is to rest the listeners.* This is an exception to the overall definition that an illustration is told to illustrate a point or an idea. But even here the illustration is not used for its own sake. It is used to give the listeners an opportunity to rest their concentration. The average person can concentrate just so long and then he needs a chance to relax. In tragic drama this is called "comic relief."

The illustrations used for this purpose need not be humorous; however, in many cases a laugh does help relaxation of tension. More frequently this use of illustration reviews or repeats the substance of ideas that have been made up to this point.

Experience suggests that the need for this type of illustration comes at what is often called "the twelve minute stretch." If you watch a group of average people gathered to hear the Sunday morning sermon, after about ten-twelve minutes into the sermon there will be a general movement throughout. They will switch sitting positions, adjust clothing, look at watches, or glance at the person beside them. This is a dangerous point in sermon delivery. You can easily lose them at this point. They have hit a plateau of their listening capacity. The speaker needs to be sensitive to this reaction and make a special effort at this point to regain their attention. Fortunately, if the speaker does move them over this plateau, there is a good chance of holding their attention for the rest of the sermon. At this crucial point an illustration is extremely helpful.

To give an example here is difficult as so much depends on the content of the sermon. Perhaps it is enough to warn the preacher that about two-thirds of the way through the sermon, this "twelve minute stretch" occurs and if a good illustration can be found to review the first two-thirds of the sermon, it will insure a more responsive congregation for the last section of the sermon.

This, however, does not limit the use of an illustration for relaxation to this particular point of the sermon's development. Depending on the content, many such illustrative breaks may be needed throughout the sermon.

In summary, the purposes of an illustration are to clarify or enforce an idea, involve the listener, or just rest the strain of concentration.

Requirements of an Illustration

There are three basic requirements for the choice and use of illustrations:

1. _Validity._ The illustration should be valid. It should illustrate the point made. The issue here is, can you illustrate a point that has not been made? Many homileticians hold that you cannot. However, there are occasions when surprise is an important element of the illustration and the point of the story would be "killed" if made first. In most instances such illustrations do not illustrate a point, as much as make the point. As with most of the parables, they are the idea that is being presented.

The important consideration is the quality of the illustration itself. Is the point of the illustration so obvious that it cannot be missed by the listeners? If this is so, it can be used as an effective way to introduce an idea to the listeners.

This applies primarily to story-type illustrations. Example pictures, similies, and metaphors should in most cases follow the point made rather than precede it.

2. *Variety*. Illustrations used in the same sermon should be varied. We all have our personal interests, and it is easy to find and use illustrations from this source alone. I once knew a preacher who loved to climb mountains. After his month's vacation in the West where he indulged in his favorite pleasure and pastime, every one of the illustrations used in his sermons for the next several weeks would be "mountain climbing stories." In fact, one of his parishioners said to me that he and his wife got to the point where they no longer said, "Let's go to church," but "Well, let's go climb another mountain today."

The best advice is to take the daily newspaper and study its layout. There are current events on the front page, then the editorials, the stock market report, sports section, household tips, games, horoscope, comics, as well as announcements of all the sales going on in town. Then look at your congregation. Some of the people will pick up the newspaper and read the sports section first. Some will turn immediately to the stock reports. Others will leaf through to find the most exciting sales. And some will go directly to the comics. This is the variety of interests that confronts you as you face a waiting congregation. The illustrations and examples in your sermon should possess the same "across-the-board" interests as the daily newspaper. Of course we can't hit all these varied interests in one sermon, but we can try to hit as many as possible.

3. *Adequacy*. The third requirement is that the illustrative material in the sermon be adequate. The speaker needs to learn to evaluate his own material in the light of experience and in the light of his own personal reaction. A tape recording of the sermon is helpful here. Record and listen to the sermon. Listen especially for the points and ideas that need more clarification or enforcement. Put yourself in the position of the listener and discover where more listener involvement is required. It will be time well spent. You

can become your own best critic, if you develop and learn how to listen. After all, we are going to preach this sermon to ourselves as well as to the congregation. Train yourself to be a good listener as well as a good speaker.

General Comments

There are some general comments that need to be made about the choice and use of illustrations in the sermon:

1. It should never be necessary to explain an illustration. As with a good joke, the point should be obvious. Students see a movie. It seems to be an excellent illustration of a point they want to make in their sermon. But the problem is that some, or many, of the listeners have not seen the movie. Therefore, to use such an illustration would be to use the unfamiliar to explain a point, which by most standards of illustration would be impossible and therefore inadvisable. It may be that enough of the movie's plot would be told that would enable the listener to follow the account and get the point. But it still remains an awkward form of illustration.

The same can be said about television programs. Here the possibility of audience exposure is broader, but we must never assume that everyone has seen the same movie or TV program we have. The best advice, when you use a movie or TV program as an illustration, is to do so as if your listeners have not seen it. Make the necessary review as brief as you can so as not to bore those who have seen it.

2. Stories and examples taken from books of sermon illustrations can be used, but in most cases they need to be rewritten in your own words. Otherwise they will sound like what they are, "canned illustrations."

Books of sermon illustrations are best used as "starters." This means that you use "canned illustrations" to get suggestions so that you may use a little imagination to create your own illustration.

The best illustrations, however, are taken from "life" and not from books. As speakers we need to train ourselves to see. We look but we seldom see. When a speaker has difficulty finding illustrative material, it is generally true that the speaker is a person with limited interests. Because of a lack of interest, we go through life looking at an illustrative gold mine of experiences and happenings and see nothing. A creative speaker who can win and move his listeners with well-chosen illustrations and examples is always a person of many interests. The personal experience is still the best source of illustrative material.

3. A warning, however. Never place yourself as the "hero" in a personal illustration. One student told that during his intern work there was an elderly lady who responded to no one on the church staff. He pointed out that he didn't give up. He made every effort to win her over, and he did. Then he added that the daughter told him that her mother remarked, "That young man taught me the meaning of the word 'Pastor'."

Now I, too, admire that young man as a pastor, but not as a preacher. A preacher, as we have noted, needs to get out of the way and let the Word come through. Likewise, when telling a personal incident or example, the speaker needs to get out of the way and let the point of the illustration come through.

There is a difference between a personal experience and an illustration of you personally. In the personal experience you are the observer of what happens. In the illustration of you personally, you are the illustration. It is the personal experience that makes an effective illustration. The personal tone of the illustration is maintained, but the illustration is not destroyed by the intervention of the teller.

There is a possible exception. And that is a personal account of a mistake you made, or a foolish thing you did. This is generally effective in establishing good rapport with your listeners, because the listeners can identify with you. And you do not interfere with the point, but are sacrificed in order that the point may be made. This can, however, be overdone. The best advice is to use personal illustrations cautiously and sparingly. Remember the definition of a bore: "a bore is a person who is talking about himself when you want to talk about yourself."

4. When using a story illustration, real integrity can be given to the story by using an image or phrase from the illustration later on in the sermon. For example: The story is told that when Sherman marched to the sea, a little old lady refused to leave her home in rural Georgia. She stood on the front porch and saw the homes and the fields of her neighbors burning across the valley. As Sherman's army came closer and finally started down the road to her farm, she was unable to stand by and do nothing. She took her broom and stood defiantly in the middle of the road.

The marching soldiers saw her and came to a halt. The captain shouted, "Old lady, do you expect to win the war with a broom?" "No," came the quick reply, "but at least I'll show the world which side I'm on."

When this illustration was used, the preacher made several references to the "broomsticks of determination" later in the sermon. That gave real integrity to the illustration and made it a vital part of the total sermon development.

5. Never apologize for using an illustration. Frequently a speaker will say, "Forive me, if you have heard this one before." My response is this: "If the story is good, and well told, it can be heard again. If it is a poor story, badly told, once is too often."

6. Important to the process of creating effective illustrations, as well as important to the whole sermon process, is the imagination.

The common understanding of imagination is generally not complimentary. We say, "It's just your imagination." And that is meant to be a put down.

Imagination from this point of view is the opposite of facts and reality. Therefore, the imagination and the material it produces is potentially dangerous to the content of the sermon where truth is an absolute. However, this is to confuse imagination with fantasy.

Imagination is a legitimate tool of all creative expression. It is the ability to put yourself into a given situation. It is the ability of being able to experience what is happening in that situation. By use of the imagination you can enter into the text and not read something into it but actually withdraw something from the text that others standing on the surface of the text cannot see. The creative sermon which results enables the listeners to see what is in the text, but which has been hidden from them up to this point. Sound advice here is that we are permitted to read inbetween the lines of the text so long as we stay inbetween the lines.

By use of the imagination, the speaker can enable the listeners to see the invisible reality of the Holy Spirit at work in the world. The imagination is not only insight; it is also foresight, enabling us to see the ultimate victory of God despite the massive negative evidence in our present-day world. Rightly used, the imagination enables the preacher to excite the listeners with the potential options for human existence now possible because of what God has done in Jesus Christ.

The Body of the Sermon

To complete the bumble bee we need a body. And that body needs an identifiable shape. In the case of the sermon this is frequently referred to as the outline. The listeners give the speaker their attention and they reasonably expect to be rewarded with a clear, coherent, to-the-point development of a theme. They do not wish to listen to scattered, unrelated ideas, no matter how profound. They demand that the body of the sermon have a shape that they can identify. To this end we create structure that the resulting sermon might have shape.

We have said that the structure of the body of the sermon depends on the sequence and value of ideas. We can think of only one thing at a time. Therefore, we need to organize our thoughts so that they will be related meaningfully and will move to one central thought.

We need also to establish what we want to see happen in the minds of the listeners. Therefore, materials need to be arranged so that they are most likely to accomplish this objective — the purpose of the sermon.

How structure is best formed and just how influential the form of the idea and the end purpose are in determining the eventual sermon structure is one of the most controversial issues of homiletical theory.

Some teachers of preaching advocate a "construction" approach. Here, ideas and materials are viewed as building blocks. The preacher is an engineer. He surveys his available ideas and studies the purpose, then devises a blueprint or an outline and proceeds to build. Ideas are bricks, support material is the mortar, illustrations are the windows. The chosen outline-design determines the use of each type of building material.

For some authorities this approach is too rigid and mechanical. Fenelon, for example, says:

> *Ordinarily they put there the kind of order that is more apparent than real. Moreover they dry up discourse and make it rigid. They cut it into two or three parts ... No longer is there genuine unity — there are two or three distinct discourses unified only by arbitrary interconnection.*

Most who object to the mechanical-outline approach suggest that structure should be more like a living organism than a building. Given a central idea, the sermon should not be built according to a blueprint, it should grow. As a seed contains the shape and design of the flower it produces, so the central idea of a sermon has the structural form inherent within it. The preacher simply enables the seed-idea to follow its own pattern of development.

All agree that structure involves sequence, and value relationship of ideas, and that the finished product should possess a unity that holds the sermon together. But the practical question still remains for the preacher, "How am I going to do this?" We have all seen too many "sermonic constructions" fall apart before we got the roof on. And we have nourished many seed-ideas that refused to bloom. It is one thing to have a sound theory about good sermon structure. It is another thing to put that theory into practice.

Structural Thinking

My own approach to teaching sermonic structure is that it depends on bringing together two things, the particular idea of a sermon and the general thought patterns of the way the listeners think.

First, there is the particular idea of the sermon. This is the central thing we want the sermon to say. As we have said, this consists of sequence and value relations of the thought-units which make up an idea. Since we are not just creating a literary work, but are communicating this idea to a listening congregation, we need to take into consideration the general thought patterns of the mind, for these are the ways the listeners think.

There are basic patterns and forms of thought. They are the "deep" structures by which the mind forms ideas. They may be inherent in the mind or they may be learned patterns. But the fact is, when we think, we generally follow certain basic forms or patterns. When these general thought patterns of the mind are brought into contact with the particular thought we wish to express, we find that there is in some cases a "fit." That is, one general structure would seem to be the best structure for the expression of our idea.

Let us identify some of these basic structures which the mind uses to organize its thinking and then see how they can and have been used to influence sermon structures. We will mention only the more familiar basic structures.

1. Problem-Solution. When the mind realizes that something is wrong, it attempts to identify the problem, define and analyze it, and then strive for a solution. The mind seldom has a solution before going in search of a problem. The natural sequence of thought is problem-solution. This basic way in which the mind thinks can be utilized by the sermon as its unifying structure. A survey of books containing written sermons will reveal that this has been a popular and successful structure for many sermons. This does not mean that a rigid outline has been superimposed upon the content of the sermon, as some suggest. Rather, it is that the idea the preacher wanted to express fit a basic pattern which was familiar to the listening mind.

The danger of the problem-solution sermon structure is that the preacher often assumes problems that do not exist, or he forces problems to fit solutions which he has found in the text. The fault is not in the structure selected but in the sermon idea itself.

Another danger of the problem-solution structure is that the problem portion of the sermon is effectively and thoroughly presented, but the solution is sketchy and weak. Pious platitudes are often presented as solutions when what the listeners want is a detailed, practical answer. Of course, it is always easier to identify problems than to discover solutions. Besides, the Bible rarely gives specific answers and detailed solutions. Therefore, the problem-solution sermon generally ends up creating more questions than satisfied solutions in the minds of the listeners.

It is not always necessary to attempt to give pat answers in the problem-solution-style sermon. We should not give the impression as we present the problem that we have all the answers ready to spring on the congregation at the end of the sermon. The most effective procedure is to view the sermon as providing various options for the listeners that will enable them to formulate their own answers. For example, our Lord ends his parable of the Good Samaritan with the Question, "Who do you think proved neighbor to the man . . .?" The options provided by the story lead to but one conclusion. However, the listener is not given an answer but is free, and not forced, to accept the solution. In a well-developed problem-solution structure, the destination is clearly established by the sermon, but the listener has the experience of arriving there by his own thought process. The structure of a problem-solution sermon, therefore, is a clear presentation of the problem, a treatment of the various options, and then a joint conclusion as to the best solution.

2. Time Sequence. The mind tends to think in the sequence of past, present, and future because this is the order of experience. One has only to read a book, or see a movie, that has a great deal of flashbacks to discover how much more difficult it is to follow the story. Such listening demands careful concentration because the sequence of happenings is not the familiar pattern of the way we ordinarily think.

The time sequence of past, present, and future can and has been used as the structural basis of the sermon.

3. Place Sequence. The mind also arranges things according to where they happen. A friend of mine returned from a world tour and invited us over to see his slides. He began showing the slides in no particular order. The first was a scene in Spain, the second a street in Germany, then a church in London. The fourth was a bridge in Spain. An hour of this experience was maddening. It was as if my mind were shouting, "Order, man! Order!" Now we can utilize this characteristic pattern of the mind to organize our thoughts around places and locations.

4. _Elimination._ Another basic pattern of the way the mind thinks is elimination. When making a decision each possibility is considered, and either accepted or rejected. Then another option is considered until the best is discovered. Say the text is from the farewell discourses of our Lord to the disciples where he says, "My peace I give unto you" (John 14:27b). The central idea of the sermon is to convey the meaning of that peace. So the structure of the sermon could be:

Point 1. It is not Fortress Peace which is established by force.

Point 2. It is not Palace Peace where we indulge ourselves with material luxuries to forget our problems.

Point 3. It is not Monastery Peace where we escape our problems by denying they exist.

Point 4. Rather the peace Christ gives brings us to a right relationship with God so that we might know who we are by learning whose we are.

5. _Logic Patterns._ The mind also thinks in the structural forms of inductive and deductive logic. The inductive pattern is that we know what is true in a number of individual cases and examples, and then move to see that an overall truth is valid.

The deductive pattern begins with a generally accepted truth and moves to specific instances and examples.

This is not something we superimpose upon the mind. It is the way the mind thinks. If the idea we wish to express and the purpose we desire to realize fit this pattern, then the sermon utilizing this form as its structure can be easily followed by the listeners.

6. _Parts of the Whole._ The mind thinks of the whole being made up of parts, and parts fitting together to form the whole. If you desire to deal with the issue of a

single idea, topic, or subject, this whole-parts pattern might be the answer. Take the word "blessing." You might divide your idea of what blessing means into three parts:

Point 1. Blessing as understood by the world is being healthy, wealthy, and wise.

Point 2. Blessing as understood in the Old Testament meant many children, good harvest and a large flock.

Point 3. Blessing in the New Testament means being called to suffer with Christ that we might share in his glory.

7. *Comparison.* The mind thinks by comparing one thing with another to discover differences and similarities. This would suggest an extended analogy structure where you consider what happened in the text and compare it to what is happening now.

There are two possibilities here. You could structure the sermon into two major divisions:

Point 1. What happened then.
Point 2. What is happening now.

Or you could deal with the text or idea step-by-step, including an analogy at each step along the way:

Point 1. Then and now.
Point 2. Then and now.
Point 3. Then and now.

8. *Meditation.* Sometimes the mind thinks by taking an idea and just playing with it, rolling it around, and looking at it from different points of view. This would suggest a structure of one single point. There would be no particular sequence of the various aspects of the central idea considered. The unity of the structure would

be maintaining the single central idea throughout the entire sermon.

9. *Narrative.* The mind thinks in the form of story. Currently much is being done with this by the narrative theologians. Here, a plot moving to solution becomes the structural form. Every good story is made up of a strong who, an interesting what, a convincing why, and a reasonable how. One or the other of these dominates and determines the plot profile of the story.

When applied to sermonic structure the sermon becomes not so much a series of points made but the movement from one point to another. The other day I was returning from our main shopping mall, and I passed by the local drive-in movie. It is notorious for its XXX-rated movies. To my surprise, two Walt Disney movies, rated G, were posted. I thought to myself, "There is a story here. Why the radical change?" Everyone in the neighborhood knows the facts. One, this is an X-rated drive-in, and two, it is now showing Walt Disney movies. The facts are obvious. They are not the story. The story lies in between the facts. How is it that an X-rated drive-in becomes a G-rated drive-in?

Structure becomes the transition that holds the facts together. We have all heard sermons that present a problem. Then in the last short paragraph the preacher proclaims with great authority that Christ is the answer. The sermon possesses all the facts but the process — the story plot — by which you move from problem to solution is neglected. The process in a narrative sermon is the structure.

Take the Parable of the Prodigal Son. It is the story of a boy who, at the beginning of the story, demands of his father, "Give me what is mine." The story climaxes with the same boy on his knees crying out, "Make me thine." The narrative approach is not to prove or defend or even to explain these radically different attitudes of the son, but to show the process by which the same young man can say at the beginning of the story, "Give me what is mine" and at the climax of the story, "Make me thine." The structure of the narrative sermon takes the listener through the development of story so that the listener can experience what happened. The structure is not so much a construction process as it is being taken on a trip.

These basic structural forms by which the mind thinks are not to be artificially superimposed upon the central idea you wish to communicate. You must never force your idea to fit one of these structural patterns. Rather, they should be placed up against the suggested structure of the sermon idea to see if there is a possible fit. They are simply traditional patterns of the way the mind thinks and the way in which many preachers have organized their sermons. When used they will be familiar structures to the listeners.

Hopefully, when all else fails, these traditional structures will enable you to find an acceptable structure for the sermon you want to write. Certainly we all strive for fresh, new, and creative structures born out of the idea of the sermon. But when the sermonic idea refuses to produce a creative structure, then we need to have at our disposal structures which have worked before.

Sometimes a happy compromise can be reached. When we place our sermonic idea up against these traditional structures a creative new way of using the traditional structures might emerge.

The essential thing is that the final sermon we develop possess a sequence of ideas that is easy to follow, the value of ideas that is readily recognizable as a unity which holds the sermon together, and a main theme that comes through loudly and clearly, and, finally, that the purpose of the sermon is accomplished and a change is worked in our listeners. We need to remind ourselves that when we say, "What is needed today is the creative sermon," we do not mean simply a sermon with a new and fresh structure. Rather by "creative sermon" we mean a sermon that does something in the lives of the listeners.

Common Faults of Sermon Structure

Before we close this discussion of sermon structure, let us look at a few common faults that prohibit a clear and sound structure.

1. Putting too many ideas into one sermon. It is much better to deal adequately with one good idea, than to try to include everything you think the text has to say.

2. Wordiness in stating the main points of the sermon. Lead details to the discussion which follows. Strive for a key word, a key phrase, or a simple sentence to carry the idea of each one of the main points you desire to make in the sermon. Think of these as signs, or symbols, of an idea rather than the complete expressions of the idea.

3. Failure to group thoughts under one main point or idea. Many times the speaker talks about something and then later brings up the same thing again and discusses it. Everything you want to say about a particular aspect of a subject should be discussed at the same time.

4. Failure to provide adequate transitions from one idea to another. (This will be discussed in detail on page 128.)

5. Lack of review and repetition. The traditional advice, "Tell them what you are going to tell them. Tell them. Then tell them what you told them," has some practical validity. In many cases, however, "telling them what you are going to tell them" at the beginning of the sermon destroys the suspense and the surprise element which can be vital to a sermon. But the advice to "tell them what you told them" is sound!

This need not be an involved and labored repetition or review. In most cases, just a sentence that recalls the thought will be sufficient. This is particularly helpful in the last section of the sermon, but it may also be needed throughout the development of the sermon.

A sermon ought to provide "whistle stops" throughout where someone who has wandered away from the train of thought might be able to get back on. A sentence of repetition or review can provide this. It will enable many a passenger to finish the trip with you.

6. *Failure to identify important points for your listeners*. If a sentence or a word is of key importance to the development of your thought, say that it is. In some cases repeat the word or sentence immediately so that the listeners cannot fail to catch that it is important. Remember that the listeners cannot read your mind; they can only hear what you say.

7. *Top-heavy structure*. The first part of the sermon is frequently over-developed in comparison to the remainder of the sermon. It is better written and more adequately illustrated than the rest of the sermon. This may be due to poor planning. Or it may be that we are fresh when we begin working on the sermon but tire of the labor and finish the rest as rapidly as possible. Or it may be due to the fact that the first part used up so much of the allotted time of the sermon that the rest had to be slighted. Strive for balance in the various divisions of the sermon.

8. *Lack of clean-cut divisions between the ideas and thoughts*. A sermon should flow, but it should not run together. The fault here generally lies in the thought processes of the preacher, who has failed to establish ideas clearly in his own mind before he began constructing the sermon. If an idea is not clear to the speaker, the preacher certainly never make it clear to the listeners.

Summary

When thinking about sermon structure, remember the bumble bee. Make sure that the sermon has a well-shaped body, an attractive head, an effective stinger, solid legs, and wings carefully chosen and fashioned to give the sermon lift and movement.

4

Marks of Effective Speaking

Speaking is one of the most ancient skills of man. Even though we have moved away from the formality of classic oratory in the direction of a more informal and conversational style of delivery, some of the basic principles of effective speaking remain unchanged and can still prove useful.

Exactness

One basic principle that remains unchanged is the need to be exact in our speaking. This is particularly true today, for we live in a world that demands that we say more and more in less and less time. This is the result of the convergence of two trends.

First, there is the development of Biblical Theology which has called our attention to the importance and the necessity of biblical preaching in our times. As pastors called to proclaim God's Word, we can no longer be satisfied with chatty little talks about religion and current events, or quaint little ethical homilies on isolated and independent texts. Today there is a need for clear, concise, organized development of the basic theological issues of Scripture and their relevance to the needs of people. There is a need to see the wholeness of the Bible's message, and to catch the total cosmic impact of the gospel in our times.

The thinking people of our parishes are also aware of this. The seriousness of life daily impresses itself upon them, filling them with anxiety and apprehension. They want to know what God thinks and what he has to say in these perilous times. They want depth and not shallowness in our preaching. They want the certainty of a divine Word. They want a voice of authority from beyond the limitations of this existence because they know that only such a transcendent Word can deliver them from a world that offers eventual destruction and death.

At the same time, this desire for solid and sound preaching converges with the practical aspects of congregational life. People want shorter and shorter sermons. This is an age of condensation. Our people live in a world of efficiency experts and continually-broken speed records. This is a time-conscious generation where everything is reduced to *Reader's Digest* size, ready-mix simplicity, heat-and-serve efficiency. Congregations today are not willing to wait patiently while a speaker finds the right word and the best way to express an idea. They want a preacher to get to the point quickly, directly, and concisely. This means that for the person in the pew, length is not a mark of strength for the pastor in the pulpit.

These two demands — depth and time — converge to present us with the need of being exact — to say more and more in less and less time.

Eloquence

Another mark of effective speaking has been eloquence. We recognize that eloquence is not a popular word today in the general field of public speaking or in the particular area of homiletics. It suggests to many a polished delivery that comes across to the listeners as artificial or even pompous. This, however, is a misunderstanding. Actually the true meaning of eloquence is discovered in that vital aspect of speaking which recognizes that people are moved to listen and react to a speaker not just on the basis of the clarity of content but by sounds which please the ear. Eloquence is the effort of the speaker not only to say something but to say it well. It is striving to create an oral production that people enjoy listening to. Phrases are balanced and words are carefully selected for their sound value as well as for their meaning. Sentences are well thought out for their oral beauty as well as their clear expression of an idea.

Paul Sherer once said to his class in homiletics, "The tragedy of modern preaching is that the men who know the gospel don't know how to preach, and the men who know how to preach don't know the gospel." Eloquence is vital to knowing how preach. It is the greatest respect a speaker can pay to the truth of the gospel.

Others react against eloquence, believing that there is no place in preaching for so obviously a human accomplishment. Preaching is an act of God and the less a person has to do with it the better. It emanates from persons inspired and empowered by the Holy Spirit. Human skills and techniques of rhetoric only stand in the way of the Word and compete with it for attention.

Technically this is known as the "mystical" approach to preaching. It takes as its authority the prophets of the Old Testament who claimed to be oracles of God. It was the message and not the speaking ability or skill of the prophets that identified them as the true voices of God. This approach was revived during the Reformation when theological attention was focused exclusively on the efficacy of the Word. The authority of revelation was to be found neither in the church as an institution nor in the clergy as heirs of the apostles; authority was in the Word and in the Word alone. Humanity was held to be totally corrupted by sin. Every area of his being was invaded and held prisoner by evil. Therefore, it followed that the less humans had to do with presenting the Word the better.

For many years this attitude has dominated most of the evangelical seminaries of Protestantism. The popular expression of this preaching philosophy is that anyone can preach as long as he is saturated with the true Word and sound doctrine. It followed that the primary task of the seminary is to teach persons who are to enter the ministry the correct interpretation of doctrine and Scripture. To know the Word is all that is necessary. Content is the only thing of importance in the sermon. The Holy Spirit working through the Word will accomplish the rest.

Therefore, the average person graduating from the seminary has had little or no formal training in speech. As a result, pastors spend most of their ministry as homiletical cripples, limping heroically but pathetically through sermon after sermon, valiantly striving but never getting off the ground of the ordinary and the mundane, never giving God the best they are capable of, never fully knowing the thrill of artistic achievement dedicated to God. This is the tragedy of modern preaching — a tragedy not due to the lack of desire, or concentration, or dedication in the part of the preachers, but due to inadequate understanding of speaking skills and techniques.

The time has come for us to face frankly the fact that this problem of the relationship of preaching to the whole discipline of public speaking has been too easily dismissed by this exclusively mystical approach. Basically the sermon is a speech. It involves a speaker, subject matter, delivery, and occasion. As such it is directly related to rhetoric. Granted the sermon is more than just a speech. It possesses a theological dimension which is pervasive and decisive in both its content and delivery. It is, as we have pointed out, God's chosen way of speaking. It is an act of grace. It is an act of the Holy Spirit. It is a vital part of the redemptive activity of God in Christ. But it is also a human activity which uses human talents and abilities. This human aspect must be recognized and considered. Paul Sherer has said:

But the kind of pious palaver which older and more experienced ministers sometimes give to the younger about not having every sentence rounded out and polished too prettily, about being altogether too careful and precise, about throwing yourself on the mercy of God and saying what is in one's heart, to me that is an abomination and it is wicked. You do not have to wait until Sunday morning to throw yourself on the mercy of God; you can do it the Monday before and have a few days in which to appropriate the mercy when it comes. [1]

What is suggested here is not a simple answer of cooperation between the preacher and the Holy Spirit. Rather, it is a situation in which the mercy and grace of God are prevenient. The words we speak in our sermons are God's before they are ours. It is not as if we could divide the honors between God and ourselves, God doing his part and we doing ours. The act of preaching cannot be adequately expressed in terms of divine initiative and human co-operation. It is false within the activity of preaching to think of the area of God's action and the area of our action being delimited by each other, and distinguished from each other by a boundary, so that the more of God's grace and mercy there is in preaching, the less it is our own personal action. The preacher is not a puppet in the pulpit, but a responsible person; and the truth is that the preacher is never more truly personal than in those moments when he or she is most completely being used by God.

Yet the divine action must always be primary and dominant over the human. What happens in the preaching situation does not have to be all God, but it must be all of and from God. God takes our limited abilities and skills into his own redemptive activity and transforms them into the instruments of his Word. The key to this relationship of human skill and divine grace is neither exclusion, one from the other, nor co-operation, man plus God; rather it is transformation. It is an experience whereby a person offers his speaking abilities and talents to God as the bread and wine offered in the communion service. God takes these earthly elements and consecrates them, transforming them into means of grace.

The skill of rhetoric is not by its nature in competition with a speaking God. It can be an art dedicated and used in God's service. The mystical action of the Word and the human activity of preaching are not exclusive one of the other. Both are a vital part of the process which is divinely ordained and which can be a divinely-operated process. That God can and does work through the stammering, rhetorically unskilled witness we will not deny. The awkward speaker has many times been used by God to accomplish heroic results. But neither can we deny that God can and does choose to work through developed and perfected human skills of public speaking. God does not detest human effort. He transforms it. He accepts and consecrates it. This is the way God works.

The words of Augustine are to the point here when he writes:

> The human and the divine acts are not mutually exclusive. God could write His message in the sky, or on clay tablets, or through the mouth of an ass, but instead He usually chooses to work through the normal, natural human processes of thought, study, preparation, voice, body, language arts, communication skills, and growth. Keep your belief in God and the mystical experience if you must but this does not mean you cannot also keep rhetoric. Your use of classical, systematic rhetoric natural and human as it may seem is not a denial of God. It is simply a recognition that God uses it and works through it. [2]

Human rhetoric must be in a sense baptized into the task of preaching. It must go through an experience of crucifixion and resurrection. It must die and be born again. It must die in the sense that we acknowledge that human rhetoric can do nothing as far as the salvation of humanity is concerned. We must recognize fully that, in and of itself, rhetoric is powerless in the presentation of God's Word. But having honestly acknowledged this we must then dedicate human rhetoric to God and his redemptive work in Christ Jesus, our Lord. Thereby, rhetoric will be resurrected to a new life of usefulness within the pulpit.

According to the sacrificial laws of the Old Testament, each offering placed on the altar of God must be perfect, spotless, without blemish. So the demand comes to us who preach on Sunday morning to offer our sermons and speaking bodies as a living and worthy sacrifice to be used by God in his redemptive action. This means we must continually strive to improve our methods of sermon writing and delivery. We must develop, insofar as we are able, an eloquence in our preaching style. The dynamic view of the Word of God can accept no less.

Naturalness

Our present age places a great stress on naturalness. The phony is quickly recognized and rejected. The listening congregation reacts warmly to the person who is open to them and presents himself as a real person. This has meant that preaching has become more conversational and informal. Naturalness, however, is not easy. Like exactness and eloquence it is a developed speaking skill.

Every good speaker must establish his own natural speaking style and then continually strive to develop and improve it. The danger in the process is that we are attracted to a certain speaker and establish him or her as an ideal model and then proceed to become an exact carbon copy. Nothing could be more disastrous for the development of a natural speaking style in the pulpit.

As we are a unique personality, so we need to develop our own unique preaching style. This does not mean that we should not study effective preachers and learn from them. We should. It is important to see how accomplished and experienced preachers handle themselves in the pulpit. However, rather than selecting one person and imitating his good points, it is best to become aware of various strong points of many good preachers. Then set about organizing these various strong points into your own personal natural style. Everything that a speaker does in the pulpit he has learned from watching someone else, but it is the selectivity and organization of styles and forms that creates the unique speaking personality.

Naturalness of style will serve as an important check on attempts to be overly eloquent — to use big words and flowery phrases. It will also help us avoid developing a pulpit tone that is artificial and offensive. In most cases, pulpit tones are developed because the speaker is attempting to imitate a speaker he has heard but who has a voice that is pitched different from his own. Voices have personalities and we should be certain that our own speaking voice fits our natural endowments. Low pitched voices with a rich, resonant quality are the most pleasant sounding in the pulpit. But an attempt to throw your voice into a range not your own is disastrous.

The danger of naturalness is that the beginning speaker will interpret it to mean being what we are and intend to remain. This is to miss the point completely. When God calls us to preach, he calls us to be what we are, but what we are _at our best._ The true meaning of the challenge of naturalness is that we should strive to improve and perfect ourselves so that the best we do comes naturally. For example, some understand naturalness to mean that we can use slang and poor English in the pulpit because this is our everyday way of speaking. This is not what naturalness means at all. Rather, the demand to be natural is an ultimatum to eliminate such things as slang and poor English from our daily vocabularies so that correct expression in our preaching becomes our natural way of speaking. Naturalness? Yes! But, like eloquence, not in and of itself. Naturalness separated from earnest, daily striving after better speech habits becomes an encouragement to vulgarism.

The sermon is a unique kind of speaking, not only because of its theological dimension as a means of grace for those who listen, but also because of its effect upon the speaker. The sermon is a dialogue between God and the listener in which the preacher remains a listener while he is speaking the Word of God. The preacher must think of himself as a witness rather than as a reporter. A witness, unlike a reporter, is involved in what he is saying. He is affected by it, modified by it, moved by it, changed by it. The tone of voice must say, "I have been caught up in this." Facial expressions and gestures must say, "I have been changed by this." The heart of naturalness in the pulpit is to be involved, to communicate to your listeners that you really believe what you are saying and at the same time you are being changed by what is being said.

Natural style in the pulpit comes from personal involvement. It must be you in the pulpit — you at your best! God does not expect that we will all be great preachers, but he does demand that we be better preachers — better than we were the last time we walked into the pulpit. This means giving our all in preparation and personal improvement. This means never being satisfied with what we have done. This means continually striving to become a better trained and equipped speaker, a more informed and coherent thinker, a more authentic person, so that when we enter the pulpit the best we are comes forth naturally.

This, then, is the simple, direct, but difficult challenge of contemporary preaching — to be exact, to be eloquent, to be natural. The question now is how.

5

Oral Style Writing

We have said that effective preaching demands exactness and eloquence. Our age adds the demand to be natural. The question therefore is how are we to develop a preaching style that is both exact and eloquent and at the same time natural? The suggestion of this book is to write the sermon in an oral style. This involves three things: (1) write a full manuscript, (2) write it in oral style, and (3) use an oral style manuscript in the pulpit.

Let me pause here and point out that I am fully aware that some people are not manuscript preachers and should not try to become such. Some few have the ability to memorize their sermons, and many preach from prepared notes. However, having taught preaching for more than twenty years, I have found that many people who use notes could greatly improve their preaching by discovering a manuscript that does not destroy the desired eye contact with listeners and gives the impression that only brief notes are being used. This is the strong selling point of the oral style format.

I do not suggest that all people should use the oral style manuscript in the pulpit. But I am convinced that a study of the oral style manuscript will help your preaching no matter what method you use in the pulpit. The oral style manuscript with its unique format gives an insight into the difference between written and spoken language which is vital to effective speaking.

Write the Sermon in Full Manuscript

If we are to be exact and eloquent in our preaching we must write our sermons in full manuscript form, even if we do not plan to use the manuscript in the pulpit. Quintilian, one of the most famous of the teachers of speech, two thousand years ago wrote in his *Institutes of Oratory:*

> ... *it is the pen which brings at once the most labour and the most profit. Cicero is fully justified in describing it as the best producer and teacher of eloquence, ... We must therefore write as much as possible and with the utmost care. For as deep ploughing makes the soil more fertile for the production and support of crops, so if we improve our minds by something more than mere superficial study, we shall produce a richer growth of knowledge and shall retain it with greater accuracy. For without consciousness of such preliminary study our powers of speaking extempore will give us nothing but an empty flow of words, springing from the lips and not from the brain. It is in writing that eloquence has its roots and foundations, it is writing that provides that holy of holies where the wealth of oratory is stored, and whence it is produced to meet the demands of sudden emergencies.*

Quintilian's central truth that writing is an essential part of good speaking has been attested to by the great speakers of every age. This is immediately apparent if we turn to the history of preaching. Pastors who have carefully analyzed their own preaching methods to help others have consistently recommended the importance of writing in sermon preparation. Their personal testimony is that every preacher would greatly improve his pulpit style, if he would submit himself to the rigid discipline of writing sermons in full. With the exception of a few gifted speakers, no person can speak extemporaneously for any length of time and avoid the repetition of phrases, overworking certain words, prolixity, rambling from one thought to another, poor and faulty transitions, and fuzzy expression of ideas.

Paul Sherer, in the Yale lectures, was strong in his stress upon the place of writing in sermon preparation. He said,

> *I would not give a brass farthing, as a rule, for a preacher who does not write out at least one sermon a week for the first ten or fifteen years of his ministry. It is discipline that no man can afford to forego.* [2]

Dr. Robert J. McCracken in his book, *The Making of the Sermon*, stresses the same idea.

> *Because preaching is an art there is every reason why the entire sermon should be written in full. This rule should obtain no matter how the sermon is delivered.* [3]

Dr. George Buttrick adds his support in his book, *Jesus Came Preaching:*

> *In this question of delivery each man must discover his own method. For us writing is inescapably part of it.* [4]

One could go on quoting one homiletician after another and the advice would be the same — *write!* This same point is emphasized by English teachers who have long stressed that writing is the only means to exactness. Since preaching deals with God's Word to be communicated through our spoken words and we are challenged to say more and more in less and less time, we must be exact. If we are to be exact, we must write.

But the advice to write sermons in full manuscript is not enough. For more than twenty years I have been attempting to teach young people in the seminary how to preach. Again and again I have found that most beginning students of preaching, when given an assignment to write a sermon manuscript, do not write out a sermon as they would preach it; rather they write an essay on the given text. They are exact, often painfully exact, but their writing lacks the natural style of conversation and the free form of direct oral address.

Preaching is basically speaking and not writing; therefore, if our writing is to have any value so far as preaching is concerned, it must be written in a style that is oral rather than literary. It must be a style that is uniquely influenced by the fact that we are writing words that are to be spoken. Just there is a style for writing essays, short stories, news, and drama, so there must be a specific style for writing the sermon.

Use the Oral Style
When You Write the Sermon

To arrive at an oral style we must realize that people do not write as they speak. There is a formality about writing, an over-consciousness of words and their correct usage which seems to limit the average person and drive him into a definite "written-to-be-read" style. How often we try to write a letter to a friend and discover that we cannot write what we want to say. We cannot force our free and informal thoughts into correct, written grammatical forms. If we could speak to the individual there would be much that we could say but somehow the "to-be-written" page stands as a barrier to our unconstrained and facile expression.

Some students of language suggest that this contrast between written and spoken language originated in the formation of the English language as a written form of communication. In the beginning, English was a spoken language only. It lived and grew as a spoken language. It was not until the time of King Alfred, just before A.D. 900, that a general practice of writing English was established. At first the English-speaking people were self-conscious of their language. So dominated by the total culture of Rome, they looked upon their own language as barbarian and believed that the classical language of Latin was the only noble and worthy method of writing.

It was not until Chaucer had lived and died and had used English as the language of his poetry that people came to realize that there was real literary value and gentility of style to written English. Charlton Laird, in *The Miracle of Language*,[5] points out that at first the primitive writers of English borrowed the grammar of the Latin language for their writing; this created a difficulty which still affects our language today.

Latin and English are different in their basic structure. Latin is an inflected language, while English is a language of distribution and relationship. English is a language which uses the place of a word in a given sentence to indicate the meaning and value of the word. A technical explanation of this difference is not in order here; it is only important that we see that this superimposing of Latin grammar upon the development of written English has many times created an artificial situation and has led to stilted means of expressing our ideas in written form.

Now who are the special villains who wished all this grammatical nonsense on us? The double negative, for instance?

Well, back in 18th century England, Latin was the language of the court and the intelligentsia. The big-wigs of the time decided to push for a "universal world grammar" suitable for all times and all languages — based, of course, on classical Latin.

The fact that its structure was radically different from English didn't faze the eager reformers in the least. So, in 1762, Robert Lowth, a pompous British divine, got out a book called, Short Introduction to English Grammar, *intended to "lay down the rules" and, in addition, to "judge every form of construction."*

The boy was his own authority. He needed no help from nobody. He said that two negatives destroy each other and make a positive. He just said it, right out of his own head and, ever since, we've been stuck with it . . .

But Bishop Lowth wasn't even a good Latin scholar. Latin and Greek, too, are full of double negatives, used for emphasis. The modern Frenchman still say, "I do not know not" [Je ne sais pas], and the modern Spaniard, "I don't see nobody" [No veo nadie] . . .

The 18th century speech dictators also invented the still observed silly locution, "It is I." Again the French — and most of the English-speaking world — say "It is me."

No wonder Edward J. Gordon, Yale lecturer, says, "Most grammar teaching has little relation to the way the English language really works," and that Henry Sweet, another scholar, observed, "Most grammar has neither usefulness or validity outside the classroom." . . .

And Charles Carpenter Fries, in his American English Grammar, *declares: "There is no necessary connection between a knowledge of systematic grammar and a practical control of English." . . .*

Today's professional writer pays no attention to grammatical gobbledegook. He's too busy writing his thoughts clearly and forcefully.[6]

This does not mean that we should throw away all our ideas of grammar and use language in the pulpit that is vulgar and incorrect just to be novel or clever; rather, it means that we must re-evaluate grammar to see it as a tool rather than as a rule, a tool that is constantly growing and changing to meet the needs of both oral expression and written forms.

There is an enormous amount of scientific information about English grammar, usage, and composition available today that will give the writer a new sense of freedom. English is a versatile language. It can be both poetic and practical at the same time. It is wonderfully free in scope and vitality. But the trouble with the average pastor or seminary student is that he is held back by a limited knowledge of grammar. He has learned the rules, but just learning the rules won't do.

In fact, remembering too many rules from school days will get in the way of a free flow of natural expression. Competent authorities in the field of English grammar point out that excessive formality is a mark of the insecure writer, the "not-quite-arrived," the "semi-accepted." Great writers are never concerned with verbal trappings; they are concerned only with expressing themselves with force and dignity that comes from using language that is natural to them. What is needed is a sound working knowledge of informal, practical English that forgets about false dignity and uses language that suits the personality of the speaker and communicates to the listener.

What we suggest, therefore, is not an abuse of grammar but a use of grammar in a far more creative way. To do this we have analyzed sermons written by creative preachers to discover those distinctive elements of expression which are oral in style. We have also studied oral expression in daily conversation and informal speaking and then attempted to transfer this style into the formal tools of written English retaining, as much as possible, the spontaneity of oral communication.

Walt Whitman wrote:

Language is not an abstract construction of the learned, or of dictionary makers, but it is something arising out of the work, needs, ties, joys, affections, tastes, of long generations of humanity, and has its bases broad and low, close to the ground.[7]

Oral writing is for people who would preach to people where they are, in words they know, in a style they understand. It is a style which is both exact and eloquent, and brings to people the Word of God which gives all the words of their lives meaning and hope. This is done by writing the way you speak and speaking what you have written. Writing gives exactness and oral style gives an eloquence that is not abstract and academic but "broad and low and close to the ground."

To be exact and eloquent is not enough; we must also be natural. To write and to write in the oral style are not enough; we must be able to deliver effectively and naturally what we have written. This suggests the use of the oral style manuscript.

Use a Manuscript that Possesses an Oral Format

All of us can cite boring examples of manuscript preaching where the speaker enters the pulpit and mumbles through line after line without expression, eyes riveted to the printed page, totally unconcerned that there is anyone in the church but himself. This is a situation to be experienced once and then avoided at all costs. But this is also true of any style of delivery that we might consider. All styles are bad if improperly done. It seems unfair, therefore, to judge manuscript preaching by its failures. Webb Garrison, in *The Preacher and His Audience*,[8] points out that the claim of writers that manuscript preaching means that the attention of the audience is drawn away from the message has never been substantiated by actual tests. It is a common assumption, but not a reliably proved one.

The history of preaching is filled with distinguished achievements in pulpit delivery where the manuscript was a basic and vital part. Jonathan Edwards, Horace Bushnell, John Henry Jowett, Phillips Brooks, Paul Sherer, Edmund Steimle are just a few of the preachers who have acknowledged their use of the manuscript. Henry Sloan Coffin, for example, in *Here is My Method*, writes:

> *I know that many prefer me to preach without the manuscript; but I also know that I say more in a given number of minutes, say it with greater precision and in defter sentences, than when I let myself go without it. No doubt there is a liberty, a face to face address, a directness that folk feel is impeded when the preacher has his manuscript. But the nervous release its presence affords, the exactness of its expression of one's thought, and [for me] the "warming up" which its carefully written sentences give me, seem of great worth . . . If one has grown excited while writing — and this is my experience as a rule — the excitement is reinduced by the manuscript.* [9]

The advantage of the manuscript is that the sermon is delivered as planned. Regardless of the physical condition of the preacher, or the distractions which may arise in the process of preaching, the minister can present the message without unfortunate omissions. Another advantage is that what the manuscript preacher says is concise and to the point. The sentences are polished and pleasing to the ear. But for me, the greatest advantage of manuscript preaching is, as Coffin points out, the freedom that it gives to the preacher to approach the pulpit without undue tension. The manuscript speaker does not have to concentrate on remembering ideas, or think ahead of his speaking to find the right word, or struggle to complete a sentence once begun. All of this has been hammered out in the study, thought out, fought out, brought into the best possible structure and form. The preacher is thereby free to concentrate on interpretation and expression.

It is true that many preachers have tried to use the manuscript in the pulpit and have found that it stands in the way of effective preaching. They tend to lean on the manuscript and end up reading it word for word. No congregation will long endure a sermon poorly read. It is the thesis of this book, however, that the disadvantages of the manuscript can be overcome by creating a format for the manuscript that will not demand the constant attention of the eyes.

If we would examine the manuscript that is ordinarily taken into the pulpit it would be obvious why it is a hindrance to conversational preaching. The manuscript would appear much like an essay. The words would be crowded together in paragraphs with no indication of the important statements or words. To keep one's place in such a manuscript demands constant attention. As a result, the congregation feels left out and neglected and blames the manuscript. They are right. Such a manuscript does stand between the pastor and the congregation and prevents the free flow of communication. But we must focus the blame where it belongs — on the type of manuscript used and not on the method of delivery. We maintain that a format for the manuscript can be devised that will enable the preacher to use it and still not destroy rapport with the listeners.

Preaching today should possess the quality and effect of real conversation. It should be lively and expressive, varied and interesting. A conversationally-spoken sentence has a ring of the genuine and the normal which an obviously-read sentence always lacks; it is without the exaggerated artificiality and the unreal monotony of mechanical reading of words. The good manuscript speaker, like a skilled reader, gives the impression that he is thinking and uttering ideas for the first time even though he has carefully prepared and written them beforehand.

Such naturalness in manuscript preaching is not so difficult to achieve as it may first appear. Planned speaking with notes and manuscript preaching differ in degree rather than in kind; the mental action involved is much the same in both. In extemporaneous speaking the preacher utters the ideas just as they are created in the mind. He speaks as he thinks and the words come forth as he thinks — a phrase here, a hesitation there, a word, a spurt of words, and so on. In delivering lines from a manuscript, on the other hand, the preacher is repeating impressions given to him from the printed page. The point at issue is that the preacher who uses the manuscript must do in reading lines what is done in direct informal speaking: just as the mind creates the thoughts as the preacher is speaking, so the mind must recreate the thoughts that are to be expressed while he is following the manuscript. The preacher must read as he thinks — a phrase here, a hesitation there, a word, a series of words, and so on.

To accomplish this, we suggest an oral style manuscript which possesses a unique oral format. The manuscript page is approached as a canvas on which oral production is reproduced in a form to suggest to the speaker the informality of the spoken words of conversation. It is not designed to be read as one would read a page from a book; rather it lies before the speaker as a prompter ready to help him when needed, recalling words and sentence structure previously prepared and written down but not demanding the absolute necessity of a word-for-word reading.

The words and phrases are arranged to give each page its own unique design or form. The words and phrases are placed on the paper in such a way that they give meaning and interpretation by their very position to other words and phrases to which they are related. This utilizes the characteristic of the mind to think in the form of symbols. A word is only a symbol which suggests an idea to the mind. This is the way we think. The oral style manuscript format goes beyond the symbolism of the word and uses the size of lines, the position of words, and the shape of the written page as a whole to form a symbolic impression and suggest to the mind the ideas and their development which are contained on any given page.

The oral style format enables the speaker to respond to reactions of his listeners, to follow through where needed, to add or subtract, to repeat or restate where the development appears to be weakest. The sermon can be delivered as planned, word for word as it is written, but at the same time the free and open style of the manuscript permits the preacher to change and alter certain words and phrases or whole sections of the sermon, at will, without losing his place in the written material of the manuscript. The oral style format permits the preacher, after having left the exact wording of the manuscript, to return to it readily and pick up a needed word or statement and continue speaking by following the exact wording of the written material.

A more detailed treatment of the oral style manuscript format will be presented in Chapter 6. At this point our only intention is to urge an open mind in considering the use of a manuscript in a completely new and different way. It is to suggest the possibility of creating a useful and unique format for manuscripts that will allow the preacher to utilize the advantages of manuscript preaching without its disadvantages. It is to maintain that a preacher can speak naturally, freely, and conversationally, that he can establish and hold a vital eye contact with his listeners, while at the same time following the carefully prepared words of a written manuscript.

6

The Oral Style Format

Stop for a moment and look at this page. It is a sheet of paper with black letters arranged to form words placed in block formations called paragraphs. The general overall appearance which you receive from this page is called the format. A margin surrounds the page, indentations and blank spaces indicate a paragraph. Capitalized letters mark the beginning of sentences and the use of proper nouns. But this is the extent to which this general format aids you in understanding and interpreting the various ideas found on this page.

Ordinarily the manuscript for a sermon would follow the same style format. Sentences would be bunched together in paragraph divisions and words would be clustered into evenly-spaced sentences. If a word were more important than another, its appearance on the page would not indicate it. It would look like any other word and one would have to read the sentence before one could determine the important words and phrases to be stressed. In reality, such a manuscript can only be read. It cannot be spoken. It is even difficult to read and demands the constant attention of the eyes. The task of oral writing is to construct a unique type of format for the manuscript that will prompt the speaker with words, phrases, and ideas without demanding the constant attention of an essay-styled manuscript.

Word-Grouping and Thought Units

Now listen to someone speak. Close your eyes and attempt to visualize a format of these spoken words as they appear in the silence of space. What is the general appearance of this mental vision of spoken words? It is apparent at once that they do not come to you as blocks of words in neatly formed paragraphs. Rather, they appear as single words or as word-groupings, because we do not speak primarily in formal sentences, and certainly not in paragraphs; rather, we speak in *word groups* or *thought units* which are determined by the meaning and interpretation of the idea we are expressing, and the practical necessity of breathing.

For example, I see a black ballpoint pen on my desk. As I look at it I am reminded of the fact that it was left in my classroom after the junior examination. To produce this idea orally I would more than likely divide it up into three or four word-groupings. The first word-grouping would be, "The black ballpoint pen;" the second, "lying on my desk;" the third, "was left in my classroom;" the fourth, "after the junior examination." The third and fourth word-groupings could be combined or not, according to how I reacted to their relationship in my oral expression of the idea. The pause would probably not be as great between the first and second word-groupings and the third and fourth as between the second and third, because I would take a breath at this point in order to continue the sentence with ease.

This word-grouping, or what is often referred to as *phrasing*, is the distinctive characteristic of oral production. It enables the speaker to divide the content of an idea into workable thought units which can be comprehended by the listener while the speaker is talking. It enables the listener to think with the speaker. At the same time, this division of word-groupings forms a thought pattern which interprets what is being said. Certain words are given greater or less value in relationship to the total idea. This makes for greater clarity of communication and enables the listener to know not only what the speaker is saying, but also how the speaker feels about what is being said.

The Line in Oral Style Manuscript

To see how this characteristic of oral speech is transferred to the written manuscript, let us begin with a statement from an Easter sermon.

It was from a graveyard some 2000 years ago that the victory of Christ over the power of death gave to the world the assurance of an endless hope instead of a hopeless end.

This statement can be divided into five word-groupings or thought units. The first thought unit concerns the place, "It was from a graveyard;" the second gives the time, "some 2000 years ago;" the third is the subject of the idea, "the victory of Christ over death;" the fourth describes what happened, "gave to the world the assurance of an endless hope;" the fifth strengthens the action by contrast, "instead of a hopeless end."

Following this analysis of how this statement will be divided for oral production, the various word-groupings will be given their own individual placement in the format. Each word-grouping will form a line when it is transferred to the written page. For example, that statement would be written as follows:

It was from a graveyard
　　some 2000 years ago
that the victory of Christ over the power of death
　　gave to the world
the assurance of an endless hope
　　instead of a hopeless end.

The advantage of this placement is not only that each word-grouping stands by itself readily available to the eye, but in addition to this, each time you need to glance down at the manuscript to catch a word-grouping it always begins at the left-hand side of the page. You do not have to search to find the first word. It is always awaiting your attention at the left-hand side of the manuscript.

Indentation

You will notice that the word-groupings are placed on lines with varying degrees of indentation. This is an additional aid to indicate the speaker's feeling about the relationship of the word-groupings that make up the total statement. It is difficult to make any specific suggestion concerning the degree of indentation, as it is so much a matter of personal interpretation. However, certain general suggestions can be made.

When we were discussing the pauses between word-groupings, we pointed out that certain pauses would be longer and more obvious than others. Word-groupings that are closely related would have only a brief pause between them. The pause between word-groupings not so closely related would be longer. This would be true particularly of the pause for breath. This variation of pauses can be indicated by indentation.

For example, in the statement from the Easter sermon, the oral placement of the word-groupings would indicate that there would be a major pause after the words "ago" and "death," and a much shorter pause after the words "graveyard," "world" and "endless hope." Let me stress once more that this is entirely a matter of personal interpretation. The detailed decision concerning indentation must be worked out by the individual speaker.

Perhaps it is important at this point in our discussion to stress this fact of the individual character of the oral style format. The process of creating an oral style manuscript must always be an individual activity. Each preacher must build and create a format that is usable for him or her. The general suggestions and basic principles which we suggest in this chapter are only guides to each speaker's working out a format that will aid him or her in the pulpit. This will require imagination and experimentation. But if the oral style format is to be workable it must be a personal creation that is helpful in the pulpit.

Variety

Oral production is commonly ruined by linking words together in similar word-groupings of the same number of words without regard for the thought pattern of the idea. This makes for a choppy, sing-songy type of production. Constituent units of a sentence or idea are seldom strung together like uniform beads, but are of varying lengths. Generally a word-grouping is three to five words, frequently it is only one word, occasionally it is as many as twelve to fifteen words. The important thing is phrasing the words in various length word-groupings as indicated by the interpretative demands of the script content and the practical necessity of breathing.

Speak While You Write

All of this may seem difficult and confusing up to this point. But if you actually speak the words while you are writing the manuscript you will find that word-groupings, variety of phrasing, and indentations become a natural process. The important thing is to imagine a congregation in front of you. Speak to them. Preach the sermon and, while you speak, write the manuscript. When you pause for thought, emphasis, interpretation, or even to breathe, start a new line. If the thought unit is a single word or if you pause between a series of words for emphasis, place each word on a separate line. For example, note the statement, "A person without God is lost, alone and afraid." Speaking this statement and following the above suggestions, it would appear on the manuscript as follows:

A person without God is —
    lost
       alone
         and afraid.

Here you have crystallized on paper how the words will appear when they are produced orally. As you speak them you will realize that they are separate units of oral production. Therefore you place them on the paper so that each unit will demand its own specific point of attention. It cannot be stressed too strongly that this can be done effectively only if you speak your statements orally while you are writing them. Otherwise your groupings will be too formalized and will not represent on the manuscript how the words will be reproduced in the pulpit.

Capitalization for Emphasis

Another important aid in designing an oral style manuscript is capitalization. This is related to the process in oral interpretation which is called *centering*. The speaker attempts to direct the attention of his listeners and to hold their attention on key words and phrases while moving more rapidly over those portions deemed to be less important. Key words which spark the memory of the speaker and form the basic structure of the listeners' intelligible understanding of ideas. They are what H. D. Allbright has called "idea-carrying words and phrases."

For example, take the Easter sermon opening statement. There is in the oral production of this sentence an expression value placed on certain words which form the interpretation and point up the basic thrust of the statement. The words "graveyard," "victory of Christ," "power of death," "world," "endless hope" and "hopeless end" are the words that will be emphasized. Oral writing indicates this emphasis by capitalizing the entire word or phrase. The statement would appear as follows:

It was from a GRAVEYARD
    some 2000 years ago
that the VICTORY OF CHRIST over the POWER
    OF DEATH
gave to the WORLD
    the assurance of an ENDLESS HOPE
    instead of a HOPELESS END.

The key words are now thrown into the immediate attention of the speaker. It is possible for the eye simply to catch the important word at a glance, remembering the secondary words without actually focusing attention upon them. In a sense, this is a form of outline or a shorthand system of conveying ideas and thought units rapidly to the speaker, and thereby enables him to maintain eye contact with his listeners while following the content of the manuscript.

Oral Markings

When reading a book, we frequently underline important statements, circle key words, and make notations in the margin. This is done not only to aid memory while reading but also to facilitate a review of the material at a later date. The markings point out at a glance the important ideas and words on a page.

This same technique can be adopted for the oral style manuscript. Important words and phrases can be underlined, key words circled, and notations made in the margin. Many students use colored pencils to accentuate contrast of underlining. Some draw arrows to indicate climax and emphasis. Others even create simple cartoons in the margin to aid their memories and make the manuscript more meaningful at a glance. For example, if a certain section deals with the cross, they draw a small cross in the margin. Anything that will help create interest and aid attention is acceptable. The manuscript is your own personal prompter and the format can be as imaginative and creative as you need it to be.

It is important to note that oral markings can be overdone. When this happens they tend only to confuse the manuscript rather than to make it more meaningful. Do not clutter the page with too many markings. However, skillfully used oral markings can be visual gestures on a page aiding emphasis, meaning, and interpretation. They are like stage directions in printed form which prompt you from the margins as you go along. They enable you to indicate how you feel about what you have written so that when you face the manuscript in the pulpit you catch some of the excitement of the original writing experience. The page becomes an animation of oral production, and not simply groups of written words. It is a personal pictorial mural of what you want to say. Such additions enable the speaker to give the impression of freshness and informality despite the fact that the individual words have been carefully and thoughtfully selected. The manuscript becomes the means by which the "perfection of art is to conceal art." (Note examples of the use of oral marking in the sermons given in the Appendix.)

Summary

In this chapter we have considered the following general suggestions for the creation of your own individually styled oral format:

1. The length of the line is not determined by the length of a sentence or the width of the paper, but is determined by the oral production of word-groupings and thought units. Each time you pause for thought, emphasis, or breathing, you start a new line.

2. Indentations indicate the relationship of one thought unit to another.

3. Variety of phrasing indicated by the interpretative demands of the sermon content and the practical necessity of breathing suggest that your word-groupings and thought units vary greatly as to the number of words used.

4. Speak the sermon vocally as you write the manuscript.

5. Use capitalization for emphasis.

6. Oral markings, such as underlining and circling, are great aids in creating an interesting and usable oral style format.

Human thought is complex and not all of its complexity can be conveyed in the ordinary style of placing words on paper. The tone and feeling of the voice, the enthusiasm and stress of one idea in relationship to another, the pause for suspense and contemplation are generally lost on the written page. The oral style manuscript attempts to answer this need by freeing the writer from the rigidity of forming ideas into word-boxes we call paragraphs, and encourages the writer to design his own format of placing words on a page. General suggestions have been given, but ultimately the usability of a pulpit-prompter, oral style manuscript will depend on the ingenuity of the writer. Study the examples given in the Appendix.

Notes on Use of Oral Style Manuscript

Before leaving this chapter, a word must be said concerning the use of the oral style manuscript in the pulpit. It is obvious that when the suggestions of oral writing are carried out, many more pages of manuscript will be required than would be the case of writing a sermon in the ordinary essay style. The average oral style manuscript is at least twelve to fifteen regular 8½ x 11" sheets of paper. It is quite a task to manage this skillfully in the pulpit. Therefore the following suggestions are in order:

Never write on both sides of the paper. This permits you to use the manuscript without turning pages over. The distraction of turning pages calls the attention of the listeners away from the speaker. The manuscript should be taken into the pulpit and placed on the pulpit desk. Then slide *page one* to the *left* so that pages one and two are showing. When you have finished page one and are using page two, slide *page two over and cover page one*, thereby revealing page three. You will always have the following page showing so when you get to the bottom of a page it is not necessary to turn the page in order to continue. You simply move up to the top of the next page on your right.

You slide the pages while you are looking at your listeners. This is most important. The attention of an audience is always drawn in the direction of the speaker's eyes. Therefore, if you look down and turn a page at the same time, it will be obvious to everyone what you are doing. If, on the other hand, you move the pages of your manuscript while looking at your audience, the movement will seldom be noticed. With little practice this can be done skillfully and will aid greatly in maintaining a successful rapport between yourself and your listeners. The congregation will not object to your use of the manuscript; in most cases they will not be conscious of the fact that you are using one at all. This is but another suggestion of using art to conceal an art.

7

The Oral Sentence

The sentence in oral writing should be brisk, forceful, pleasant, and personal. It should be a unit of talk frozen into words upon a written page. When it is read it should speak, and when it is spoken it should be living conversation. This is not an easy task, but there are certain suggestions which will help develop an oral orientation to your written sentences.

One has only to turn to a book of sermons by A. J. Gossip, Peter Marshall, James Stewart, Helmut Thielicke, Edmund Steimle, or David A. Redding, and study the sentences they use to find a gold mine of model sentences with an oral style orientation. These men write sentences that leap from the page and carry you in wild excitement through the picturesque journey of their thoughts. Sometimes the sentences are long, pyramiding one thought on top of another, lifting you step by step until from the mountain of phrases and words you catch a panoramic view of the total theme. This may be followed by a short sentence that cracks like a whip across your mind, or drives into your heart like a blade of cold steel. Always fresh, these sentences flow before your mind, and you leave the sermon longing for more.

We cannot all write like a David Redding or a James Stewart, but we can all learn from them. We can learn to evaluate and appreciate the power of sentences orally oriented and we can, if we are willing to work at it, catch the spirit of the writing, and in the light of its suggestive power improve our own expression. To guide you in such a study, the following suggestions are made:

1. Develop the Short Sentence Style

The short sentence is like a snowball rounded and packed for throwing. The words are carefully chosen. They are direct and to the point.

There is little doubt that one of the greatest bars to clean oral sentences is wordiness. Words that add nothing to the clarity or power of a sentence only stand in the way of direct personal communication. They make the manuscript clumsy, fuzzy, and confused.

One of the greatest skills in the art of sermon writing is the skill of omission — the ability to cut and prune what you have written. The courage to throw out words and sentences and even paragraphs where necessary is the beginning of great oral writing. The trouble is that everything we write becomes our own little brain-baby. We have gone through the labor and pain of its creative birth, and we hate to see it dissected and torn apart. Words become our masters. The only way to save ourselves from such a fate is to test each word written to make sure that it is absolutely necessary.

The best test of the oral short sentence is to see if you can deliver it in one breath. If you can, it is rounded and packed and ready for throwing.

Look at the following passage:
"We too soon submit meekly to the inevitable.
        And think to ourselves.
                This acceptance of things as they are,
                This giving up without a fight,
                This resignation —
                        is a mark of Faith.
In the New Testament sense of the word —
        This is not faith.
        This is fatalism.
        Faith doesn't give up, or resign.
        True faith struggles and fights.
Fatalism sees things as they are
                and meekly accepts them.
Faith sees things as they should be — and can be.
        And fights to make them so.
Faith is not resignation.
Faith is determination."[1]
Note the briskness and directness of these sentences.

There is no wordiness here. Each word stands unchallenged. Each word plays its part in the total impact of the thought. Such sentences are not only pleasing to hear but a delight to preach. They almost speak themselves.

2. Build the Pyramid Sentence

The advice to develop the short sentence style must not be misunderstood. It does not mean that every sentence must be shortened to the point where it can be delivered in one breath. This would create an artificial and choppy expression of thought. The sermon would end up sounding like a page from a first reader: "This is a boy. The boy has a dog. The dog is black." By the short sentence style we mean dividing ideas into direct word-groupings or thought units which can be understood by the listener while the preacher is in the process of speaking. The formation of a sentence is after all only a grammatical decision. In most instances the same thought could be written in one complex or compound sentence or several short ones. Often it is only a matter of punctuation.

It is possible, therefore, to maintain a short sentence style even in the grammatically constructed compound and complex sentences. What happens is that the long sentence is broken down into speakable units; for example, what we would call the pyramid sentence in oral writing.

To construct a pyramid sentence the speaker chooses a series of words or phrases and presents them one after another to expand or deepen the idea. The sentence seems to grow before your eyes, unfolding itself, wider and wider, step by step, all the while carrying you rapidly and deeply into the speaker's meaning and purpose.

In the following paragraph from Edmund Steimle's Easter sermon, note how he utilizes the technique of pyramiding phrases, one on top of another, to build to the climax of his idea:

Certainly, there was no inevitable happy ending for those eleven disciples on that first Easter. Instead of going to bed to dream how nice it was that everything worked out right in the end, it drove spurs into them, goaded them into action, gave them courage and power, and for all of them no happy ending, either, no escape but rather stonings, mobs, imprisonments, death — and yet with a song all the way through to the end.[2]

Here is another example of a pyramid sentence, written by David O. Woodyard in *Living Without God Before God:*

If there has been a moment in which you were grasped by a human face as human, forgetting its color, the beauty or ugliness of its features, the differences of age, strength, and knowledge, then you have experienced "the new being."[3]

Not all pyramid sentences are this long. Many short sentences may build a climax through the use of the pyramid technique. Here are some examples from sermons of James Stewart and Arthur John Gossip:

They thought they had God with His back to the wall pinned, and helpless and defeated.[4]

What is the point and peak and heart and center of it?[5]

This is our aim, our duty, our glorious destiny, if we will take it.[6]

Such sentence structure in the writings of great preachers is endless. The pyramid sentence not only serves to build climax but communicates excitement and interest as well. It gives the impression that there is so much to say that sentences are battlegrounds in which ideas and images fight to enter in and add to the expression. These sentences come like tidal waves in the body of sermons, carrying listeners higher and higher upon their crest, speeding them toward an idea that, like a rock, will dash their smug self-satisfied minds to pieces and reshape their thinking by tearing their old ideas loose and carrying in the fresh, new enlightening ideas of the speaker.

3. Don't be Afraid of the Incomplete Sentence.

From the time we first begin to study English grammar we are indoctrinated with the principle that every sentence must have a subject and a predicate. Later we learn that there are elliptical and fragmentary sentences, but the rule of the complete sentence is so ingrained within us that we seldom write a sentence that does not have the subject and predicate carefully and clearly stated.

When we speak, however, this is not the case. We frequently imply either the subject or the predicate and in some cases both, because of the rapport of communication and understanding that exists among the minds in a conversational situation. There is a continuity of thought which carries through a conversation and completes in the mind of the listeners the fragmentary statements of the speaker.

In addition, the action or gestures of a speaker can provide the needed subject or imply a verbal action. For example, you offer a cup of coffee to a person and ask, "Coffee?" He replies in the affirmative, "Thank you." Then you might ask, "Cream and sugar?" The answer comes, "Neither." Here is an entire block of conversation without one complete sentence. To fill in or complete the statements to form sentences would destroy the conversational freshness of these elliptical expressions.

The same continuity of thought that we find in ordinary conversation exists in a well-delivered sermon.

The subject or verbal action of a sentence can carry over into an elliptical or fragmentary statement that might follow and complete its meaning. This is our natural way of speaking, particularly when we are enthusiastically involved with a subject of mutual concern to both speaker and listener.

For example, here are some fragmentary statements from the sermons of Gossip, Karl Barth, Schlink, and Steimle:

And what amazing things are offered to us on these easy terms! God's most, God's best, God's all![7]

Better perhaps, or worse perhaps. But not the same.[8]

He will abundantly pardon. Abundantly.[9]

For he came down from heaven, not to do His own will but the will of Him that sent Him; and this is the will of Him that sent Him, that, of all that He has given Him He should lose not one. Not me. Not you.[10]

He saved others, Himself He cannot save. Precisely so.[11]

The chosen one of God who would bring legions of angels to establish the kingdom of Israel as God's kingdom forever and ever . . . Today! Any moment![12]

The incorporation of these elliptical and fragmentary oral statements into sermon writing creates a sparkle to expression and establishes a distinctive oral style to one's writing. The advice, therefore, is *write as you speak*. Do not eliminate fragmentary statements from your manuscript simply because they are not complete sentences. Use them!

4. *Use the Interjection.*

The interjection, though similar to the incomplete and fragmentary sentence, is technically a principal part of speech. The interjection is an exclamatory word or statement which has little or no connection with the remainder of the sentence. It is used to add power and vitality to an expressed idea. The most common words so used are "Oh," "Ah," and "Well." They are frequently used by pulpit greats and in each case they give a personal authenticity to what is being said. For example, here is a sentence from one of Dr. Thielicke's sermons:

> *And we — well, we could then be new free persons.* [13]

And here is a sentence from Dr. Steimle's Easter sermon:

> *Well, what would you have said? Excitable women, no doubt, nerves overwrought, given to seeing things that aren't there, hearing voices no one else hears.* [14]

Such writing is conversational. The style is familiar and personal.

David Redding uses interjection phrases in a most effective way. In many cases they appear as an aside made to the congregation while he is in the process of a thought. Here are a few examples:

> *What a strange place to find a demoniac — in church! — although some critics feel the devil is safest in that sleepy atmostphere.* [15]

> *We know that floating on the water is all a matter of faith — that's how flying started, too — but the*

feat that night was not working miracles with water, but with Peter. [16]

The disciples disarmed the devil with honesty — they were always good at that — not only confessing how bad they were, which is common, but how green. [17]

Here the phrases used as interjection statements are related to what is being said and add thoughts to an idea without the structural complications of injecting a complete sentence. This makes for speaking that is less mechanical and more natural and conversational.

5. Place Key Words in Positions of Emphasis.

The sentence, like the theater, has its spotlight. It possesses a focal point of attention and the word or word-grouping which is most important to your thought should be placed in this spotlight of effective attention. The last word in a sentence or word-grouping is the last sound unit heard by your listeners and therefore stands out from all the rest. One might picture speech as shooting words out into the silence of space. As the words strike the silence they come forth as clusters, rapidly spoken, close together, or as separate word sounds surrounded by frames of silence. If you produce a cluster of words and then pause, the next word spoken seems to stand out in the silence all by itself demanding attention.

For example, here is a sentence from a sermon by Dr. Steimle:

Here in Palestine was a man who lived the Sermon on the Mount first. [18]

Now note the sentence could have been written:

Here in Palestine was a man who first lived the Sermon on the Mount.

Placing the word "first" at the very end of the sentence makes this a far more powerful and effective oral sentence. Try speaking the sentence out loud and pause before you say, "first." Notice how the word seems to linger in your ears long after you have spoken it.

This effect is created not only by the fact that the important word has been placed in the key position at the end of the sentence but also because of the pause which creates an added emphasis to the word that follows it. This same effect can be accomplished in a word-grouping. The last word spoken is the word that demands attention. Of course, volume is the most common interpretative means of conveying emphasis, but the position of the word in an oral sentence should also be considered.

6. The Balanced Sentence is Pleasing to Hear and Invites Retention.

In preaching we strive to say what we have to say in as pleasing a manner as possible. We are also concerned that people remember what we say. It isn't enough just to make a *good* impression; we desire to make a *lasting* one as well. One of the effective methods of constructing sentences to fulfill these two desires is the balanced sentence.

The balanced sentence is one which places similar or contrasting ideas into matched words or phrases. This can be done by using words that have the same sounds or word-groupings that possess similar rhythm. The structure of the balanced sentence adds color to what is said, invites attention, and aids the mind to remember. Here are some excellent examples from the Bible:

> *The foxes have holes*
> *and the birds of the air have nests*
> *but the son of man*
> *hath no where to lay his head.*
> [*Matthew 8:20*]

for there is nothing covered
that shall not be revealed;
and hid
that shall not be known.

[*Matthew 10:26*]

He that findeth his life
shall lose it;
and he that loseth his life
for my sake
shall find it.

[*Matthew 10:39*]

Here are some other examples of the balanced sentence found in outstanding sermon writing.

Simon ceased to be
Peter was being born.

[*Peter Marshall*] [19]

If God is not Lord of all
He is not Lord at all.

[*Dr. Lenski*][20]

There is nothing you can do to make God love you
more, and there is nothing you might fail to do
that would cause him to love you less.[21]

The balance of these sentences is achieved not only by the similarity of words, sounds, and rhythms but also in the skillful comparison of ideas. This is not easy writing, but it is great oral writing that is easy to speak, pleasant to hear, and a pleasure to remember.

7. The Sentence of the Pause and Double Emphasis is Unusual.

Repetition is an important part of memory. In oral writing it is fundamental, because the listener does not have the reader's privilege of going back and re-reading. But repetition can also serve to emphasize ideas and add a suggested feeling of emotion and vital concern. This is particularly true of the oral sentence which possesses the pause and double emphasis. Here the speaker pauses deliberately on a word and then repeats the word and continues the thought.

Such sentences are, for the most part, constructed in the process of speaking. We would not normally write such sentences in an essay or term paper, but they are most appropriate for oral writing. Here are some interesting examples from Gossip's writings:

Of course it hurts, hurts terribly. [22]
For always, always, they lived with terror brooding over them. [23]

Since you and I, yes you and I, can be of a like service to Him still. [24]

Here is an example from Thielicke:

Then all will be changed and everything will be different, utterly different. [25]

Notice the emphasis that such construction gives to the expression of an idea. These sentences carry an expression of concern and feeling that could have been achieved in no other way. Yet at the same time the style is natural and conversational. It is truly a bit of talk frozen to the paper, ready to come alive again in oral presentation.

8. State the Sentence in the Form of a Question.
Many times the sentence that you write for your manuscript can become more powerful if it can be made more personal. A technique for making sentences more personal is to place them in the form of a question. A

question is always directed to someone. The listener feels as if he is really being included in the conversation. At the same time, it is a compliment to the listener for it implies respect and concern for his opinion.

9. Put People into Your Sentence Writing.

Time magazine was established on the principle that human interest makes news live. The editors, therefore, present problems and events not as abstract happenings, but as the living experiences of people. Every object of the news must be related to people: what they are doing, what they are thinking, how they are involved emotionally with the events of history. This is pursued on the basis that people are primarily interested in other people, that the world in which we live is first a community of fellow beings rather than an arena of developing ideas.

The same principle is to be found in the treatment of the major points of revelation within Holy Scripture. Ideas and concepts are always presented embodied in the activities and characters of people. Faith is not defined as a theological term in dogmatics; rather, it is dramatized in a trusting father named Abraham who takes his son by the hand and leads him up a mountain, ties him to the altar, and raises a knife ready to sacrifice his most precious possession in obedience to God. Or it is personified in a centurion standing with certainty before our lord saying, "I know that all you have to do is say the word and my servant will be healed."

Devotion is not discussed; it is simply pictured by a woman kneeling before Christ washing his feet with her tears and drying them with the hairs of her head. When asked to define who is our neighbor, Christ answers with the unforgettable character of the Good Samaritan. When our Lord desires to tell of God's forgiving love, he immortalizes it in the images of the lost coin and a woman with broom in hand sweeping the floor, or the sheep lost from the flock and the shepherd endlessly searching for it, or a prodigal son and a waiting father.

There is little doubt that the universal appeal and strength of the Gospels down through the ages has been this person-centered concern of their message. They are not theological discussions of abstract virtues and ideas; they are the story of the incarnate God and daily dramas from the lives of ordinary people that march across the pages of Scripture, people who come alive and tell their stories not only by what they say, but also by who they are and the change that happens in their lives when Christ the incarnate God touches them and makes them new.

Now our sermons in like manner must be made alive not by abstract definitions and discussions but by bringing people into our ideas and sentences. This is not so much a technique of sentence structure as it is an attitude and set of mind that the writer possesses as ideas are formed into oral expression. It is important to think, while you write, in terms of people rather than ideas and concepts: doubt is Thomas extending his fingers toward the wounds of Christ; repentance is Peter kneeling in a pile of fish crying out, "Depart from me!" Courage is Stephen calm and trusting while flying stones cut into his flesh; conviction is Paul writing about the glorious news of freedom from behind prison walls.

Great oral writing is born in catching the vision of theology in action and communicating this vision personally and directly to the men and women who gather before you each Sunday morning. It is not choosing a "subject" and then developing it in three schematic divisions. It is not dealing with truth as one would with a cadaver upon a lab slab dissecting it for scientific interest. It is not speaking in a vacuum, crying out in the wilderness and darkness, caring little whether anyone hears you or not. No! Preaching is speaking to people, face to face, eye to eye, the message of the God who acted in Christ Jesus and who even now is redeeming and transforming all who listen in faith and in the presence of the Holy Spirit.

Where there is no listener there is no sermon, no matter how beautifully written or structured the script may be. Therefore, people must be written into your manuscripts. They must dominate your thinking and become as much a part of the structure of your sentences as the words you use to express your ideas. People must be in, with, and under each word you write and each idea you develop.

A person may write an essay even when there is no one to read what he had written, for content is his only concern. But not so with the person who is writing a sermon. To speak without a listener is a denial of the very nature of the act of speaking and to write a sermon without people in mind every step of the way is a denial of your call to serve. Oral writing demands that everything you write is to people, for people, about people. This is what makes the sentence truly oral in style; such oral sentences create a manuscript that is beneficial to the preacher in the pulpit and, when spoken, do glory to God who died and gave himself for humanity.

10. Throw the Sentence into the Dramatic Voice.

The dramatic voice is the direct quotation of what has been said rather than an indirect statement concerning it. This is the method of dialogue. It is the particular style of the dramatist. The person discussed is permitted to speak for himself. It is effective in oral writing because there is a freshness and an immediacy about the direct quotation that is lacking when the same idea is expressed in the third person. The speaker identifies himself with the person he is discussing and takes the listener to the original source of the idea. This helps make the sermon an experience of participation rather than an experience of looking on.

It is a simple technique, but over the years I have been impressed with how seldom the beginning student of preaching uses the direct quotation in his sermon writing. Perhaps it is the fear of being too dramatic, certainly a legitimate fear. However, the advice to use the dramatic voice does not imply a theatrical performance in the pulpit where the speaker impersonates dialects and reproduces the full gallery of expressed emotions. Admittedly this can be done by a few, but should be avoided by most. What is suggested is a sensitive interpretation to words spoken by another so that these words come alive and speak in the contemporary situation.

A common fault of the preacher is that he tends to talk about God, rather than letting God speak directly through him. For example, a student ended a sermon in the following manner:

> *Therefore do not be afraid, but be assured*
> *that God loves you, and that he will be with*
> *you in every hour of need.*

Placed in the direct form of the dramatic voice, the same message could be more powerfully proclaimed:

> *Therefore this very moment God says to you,*
> *"Be not afraid. I love you, and I will be*
> *with you in every hour of need."*

In this form the preacher has permitted God to use his voice to speak directly and personally to the listeners. It is an awesome responsibility to stand in the pulpit and have your words become the words of God himself to people. Yet to this end we have been called, to be God's voice in this time and in this place.

11. Repeat Key Sentences for Emphasis and Sequence.

A vital use of the key sentence is a repetition for emphasis and sequence. In formal oratory this is called "iteration," which is defined as the repetition, in a different form, of the controlling ideas in a sermon. The preacher knows from experience that he must repeat important points if the listener is to catch and retain the continuity of what is being said. Once a word is spoken it is gone. Therefore, repetition is essential in oral writing if the listener is to travel with the speaker through the development of ideas.

This does not mean that the main ideas are to be repeated by using the same sentences over and over. In some cases, this may be effective, particularly where the key sentence has been made emphatic by word placement, balance, or converted order. But in most instances repetition is best accomplished by pure iteration which stresses the fact that the idea or statement is repeated using new wording.

Another way to secure continuity is to use the key sentence to review or "pick up stitches." In formal oratory this is referred to as "iteration for summary and transition." When you have finished the first point of the sermon you repeat its key sentence before moving to the second point. When the second point is finished, the key sentences of both the first and second points are repeated before moving to the third point. This is best described as "picking up stitches," for in a very real sense this procedure knits the ideas of the sermon into a carefully recognizable pattern. Each time you are about to mention a new idea you remind the listeners where they are in the logical progression of the sermon theme.

This type of preaching is effective, powerful, and convincing, because it is clear; it convinces your listeners that you have something vital to say and will not risk the chance of their forgetting it. I warn you that there will be those who will tell you that such obvious presentation of structure will insult the intelligence of your listeners. For some of your listeners this will be true, yet we must remember that we preach not to impress some few intellectuals but to feed hungry souls who desire to hear the Word of God. This demands above all else that we be clear. It is not necessary to avoid the deep and difficult issues of Scripture, but it is necessary to make sure that they are made understandable for the most humble minds.

12. Build the Sentence of Transition Carefully.

One of the greatest problems of the person who speaks from limited notes is the problem of transition. The outline presents the main points and subpoints, but the movement from one point to another is often awkward. To trust the impulse or inspiration of the moment to carry the thought clearly over into the following ideas is extremely dangerous.

In my experience of reading and criticizing hundreds of sermons by seminarians, the most common fault is that the logical progression of a sermon is absent not because the points are not clear or specifically stated, but because continuity is lost in the process of moving from one point to another.

The point of transition can be likened to a ditch or a ravine. To the speaker this is no real problem; the flow of ideas is clear within his mind; the relationship of one idea to another and to the general thrust of the sermon is obvious. But the listener is attempting to follow the thinking of the speaker only on the basis of what he says. Therefore the listener becomes bogged down in the transition ditch. It would not be so bad if the speaker would pause and permit the listener to recall and think his way out, but the speaker moves rapidly to the next point and its development. "Meanwhile, back in the ditch" the listener gives up all hope of continuing. He is lost, and from this point on the sermon is a solo flight of the preacher.

As speakers we are morally bound to build some sort of passage over these transition ditches. We must inform the listeners of the total process of our thinking. We must let them in on everything that is happening within our minds, no matter how obvious. The transition statement is, therefore, not only morally necessary; it is absolutely necessary if there is to be complete communication between speaker and listener.

There are two types of transition statements. Each presents a method of lifting people over these transition ditches. The one is a *jump* statement which bluntly informs your listeners that you are going to move to another point and they should make the leap with you. The jump statement may be a connective, such as: conjunctions (and, but, or, for, because, if, unless, until); conjunctive adverbs (however, consequently, moreover, nevertheless, then, so, yet); transitional adverbs (similarly, contrarily, likewise, first, second, finally). Or the jump statement may be a transitional phrase, such as: my next point is, in the second place, on the other hand, by the same token, at the same time, this brings us to.

The second type of transition is the bridge statement. This is a complete sentence constructed to show in as smooth a way as possible the movement of thought from one idea to another.

For example, one of my students was writing a sermon on the demands of discipleship. He was pointing out how, as a young man, he had looked at the attractive poster of a Marine. He dreamed how he would look in this handsome uniform. He joined and discovered that he didn't wear this beautiful attire on the mudsoaked invasion beaches. The student desired to move from this illustration to the setting of the text where Jesus was pointing out to his followers the hardships of being a disciple. The statement which he finally used was a bridge sentence:

Just as I came to realize
that there is a vast difference
between the glory and recognition of wearing a
*   uniform*
and the grueling responsibilities of being a
*   Marine,*
so the disciples had to learn
the difference between walking with Christ
and carrying his CROSS.

The bridge sentence is built from both sides. The idea of the previous point must come forth and meet the point that follows. This can be done in one complete sentence, as illustrated, or in two carefully worded sentences which fit together to form the bridge of thought. Such sentences are not easily constructed on the spur of the moment. They require a study of the problem involved. They require planning and preparation. Look, therefore, to the sentences of transition; think them out carefully; write them out clearly; deliver them forcefully. They are absolutely essential for the logical progression and continuity of the sermon. If the outline is the structure that shows the listeners where they have been, where they are, and where they are going, the transition is the structure that enables them to travel with you when the going gets uncertain.

Summary

We have suggested these special sentences not with the idea that the beginning student of preaching should mechanically attempt to make every sentence of the sermon a balanced, pyramid, or a question sentence. The value of these suggested sentences is found in their contrast with other sentences in the sermon and the resulting variety. We have presented these sentences as examples of oral style, guides to what can be done to give sentences an oral orientation. The important thing is that the preacher should catch the spirit of these sentences and develop a taste for that which is oral.

Each individual must build an oral style of his own. You should constantly listen to the way outstanding speakers express themselves, how they use words and build sentences; develop an ear for spoken English; read plays and speeches; discover the distinctive qualities of oral writing. When possible, record your own sermons in the actual preaching situation. Study the recording with your manuscript before you, note where you left the actual wording of your manuscript, try to discover why you made this change. Note the difference between what you wrote originally in your manuscript and what you actually said in the preaching situation. Use this information to improve your sermon writing and make it more oral in style. This will not be easy, but one thing is certain: Once you have developed a style of writing that is oral and personal you will find that the manuscript, rather than being a hindrance, will enable you to speak from the pulpit with confidence and force.

8

The Spoken Word

Jesus wrote no books. He trusted his words to those who would hear and believe. His words were simple and direct, but powerful. They were words from God, words of comfort, forgiveness, and love. But most of all they were living words that had within them the power of life. They came from the living God into a dark and dead world and gave light and life. They continue to come from this living God into a world hungry for life and by these words Christ is born anew into the hearts of people in every generation.

We who enter the pulpit to preach stand in the heritage of these words — words living on the lips of martyrs, whispered by slaves, proclaimed by reformers, constantly witnessed to by his followers. These words are our heritage as preachers and heralds of God.

But this is no easy task. Christ's words must become our words. They must be communicated to our age in the words of our age. This means that we must not only be saturated with the living Word of God but we must at the same time be master craftsmen of the words of English speech. For by our words we are judged. Christ said, "I tell you, on the day of judgment men will render account for every careless word they utter; for by your words you will be justified, and by your words you will be condemned." (Matthew 12:36)

Careless words! What greater condemnation can be leveled at modern preaching? How often we have entered the pulpit with flimsy outlines and vague concepts, and attempted to feed those who hunger after righteousness by giving them God's Word clothed in the careless words which we muster forth on the spur of the moment. We struggle to find the right word, fail, yet talk on, hoping beyond hope that somehow the Holy Spirit might work despite our stumbling efforts. Afterwards we rationalize with ourselves that God does not demand great preaching, only sincere effort. Then, going back to the daily routine of the week, we neglect our study, shirking the grueling task of sermon preparation, waiting, always waiting for an inspiration. The weekend comes, finds us burning the midnight oil, searching for something, settling for anything. This is the tragedy of modern preaching — the tragedy of God's Holy Word clothed in the careless words of those who are called to preach. It is the tragedy of those who fail to see that preaching is one of the most exacting and demanding challenges of our age.

Oral writing takes seriously Christ's warning judgment against careless words. It strives for the correct word, the word that will be best understood and convey God's Word in the most vivid and valid sense. But more, oral writing considers that the words of the preacher are spoken words, sounds with meaning. Therefore, the demand is even greater upon us. Not only must the word be correct and meaningful, it must also be attractive to the ear, for we strive not only for clarity but we strive to invite attention and encourage people to listen to us.

Now it is not the intent of this book to review the basic rules of diction. There are many books at the disposal of the average pastor which have done a far more thorough task than this author could even attempt. We are concerned only with pointing out the specific oral value of certain classifications of words and how they can be used to improve our sermon writing.

1. Words of Clarity

"I had rather speak five words with understanding that I might instruct others also, than ten thousand words in a tongue." (1 Corinthians 14:19) There is no better advice for a person who would preach than these words of Paul. This is the challenge of Christian witnessing: not just to repeat what has happened but to proclaim it with clarity so that all who hear might understand and believe as well.

Luther referred to the sermon as the *monstrance*. Behind this illustration is the pertinent and direct call of the entire Reformation movement, "The Word of God *for the people*." The monstrance is used in the Roman Catholic Church in the service of the mass. It is a gold and silver vessel with a transparent section in which the host is carried in procession and exposed for adoration during the mass. In Luther's day the service of worship was a mystery hidden behind a veil of Latin verbiage and superstition. But one thing the people knew: There was a moment in the service of the mass when a miracle took place and the bread was changed into the Body of Christ. This they could understand because they could see it. As the priest elevated the host within the monstrance, the people would cry out, "Lift it higher! Lift it higher!" They wanted the priest to lift it above his head so that they might see through the window of the monstrance and view the Body of Christ.

When Luther used the monstrance as an illustration of the sermon, he was saying that the sermon, like the monstrance, should be a vessel of transparency that lifts Christ up for all to see. It is an act of clarification. This means that the sermon must not only consist of clear and inspired ideas and thoughts in the mind of the preacher, that the sermon must not only possess the true and living Word of God, but also that this Word must be held up in such clear and transparent words by the preacher that all the people might see and believe.

Today many of our sermons are mysteries hidden behind the intellectual verbiage of the clergy. As Halford Luccock pointed out, in many of our Protestant churches every Sunday is Ascension Sunday. The preacher enters the pulpit with the Word of God veiled behind professional words and ascends right over the heads of the congregation. Literally we exercise a kind of verbal excommunication by using theological terms and words that are foreign language to the average person. Every profession has words and terms that are peculiar to that profession. These words are short cuts to save lengthy explanations; but to the person outside, these same words are barriers to understanding and communicate nothing except the fact that he is completely excluded from entering in. We shall soon find, however, that these words are many times necessary if we are to deal with the live issues of Scripture. The question then is: When and how are we to use them?

There are several basic suggestions that can be made concerning the clarity of words in the pulpit.

Use the Simple Word

Whenever there is a choice of words, choose the simple one. There is a great temptation when we are preaching to use words that might demonstrate our extensive vocabularies. After all, we are human and our pulpit ambition can easily trap us into using words that will impress rather than express. But as pastors we must fight such temptations and strive for clear, simple words, even though they may not show us off to best advantage. Preaching is communication. If we are to communicate, we must be understood. If we are to be understood, we must use simple words.

Strive for Fresh Words

Experience teaches us that a sermon of simple words used in the same old way Sunday after Sunday can prove boring to a listening congregation. It is good, therefore, to strive for fresh uses of old words. The average listener tends to associate certain words with certain ideas. When we preach, our words fall into such similar phrases that, after a while, the congregation can complete a sentence once we have begun it. Try changing words about and use a word where it isn't expected. For example, look at the freshness of words and their use as they appear in this statement:

> Two thousand years ago
> Jesus Christ was crucified by the Roman police.
> Do you know what his last few days were like?
> Twelve rugged men ate supper with him
> in a little room
> with a dusty floor.
> They dipped chunks of bread
> in a pan of gravy.
> They swallowed cups of wine together.
> The next day he looked down at them from a
> cross.
> His body was broken;
> His blood poured out on the ground.
> Jesus Christ was dead!
> They were dead!
> They could no longer catch men —
> only fish!

This was written by a junior in the seminary. It is fresh and alive. It takes simple, familiar words like police, floor, gravy, and catching fish and uses them in an unusual way. Such writing takes time and effort, but it saves time and effort in the pulpit, and in the end marks the difference between ordinary and great preaching that catches hold of people's imagination and drives God's living Word deep into their souls.

Double-Barreled Words

Words are unpredictable. To the writer as well as to the speaker, this is a fascinating but exasperating fact. No word ever means exactly the same thing to two different people, because of the way in which words are learned. They are shaped and formed by our experience and none of us has had identical experiences. In general, the word may mean the same but the decisive connotations, the overtones which so drastically color our understanding can completely frustrate a speaker's desire to communicate clearly to his listeners. There is no way of preventing a listener from reading his own meaning into the words we use; but every speaker can be aware of the particularly difficult words, double-barreled words which change their basic meaning because of their current and specific use.

If you desire to know the meaning of a word, go not to the dictionary alone, but read the newspapers and watch television. These are the channels that give many words their specific meaning today. These are the powerful voices of our generation which shape the thinking of those who come to listen to you. It is this popular use of words, correct or not, that establishes current interpretation.

Abstract words in the language are more inclined to be double-barreled and to be interpreted in different ways. Take, for example, the words love, freedom, truth, peace; these are dangerous words for clear communication. To stand in the pulpit and say that God is love to people in whose minds love is a romantic Hollywood commodity, a censored emotional expression of sex, is certainly not getting across the message of the Bible. Or to say, "If Christ makes you free, you will be free indeed," in a society where freedom means the right to vote and express one's opinion, where freedom means democracy, is certainly to give the wrong impression of what Paul means when he speaks of freedom in Christ. Or to quote Christ, "My peace I give unto you," for people who are looking for escape from suffering, peace of mind, and an easy way out of facing the realities of the world, is to corrupt the meaning of Christ's words.

If we are to preach today, communicating God's Word in the words of our age, we cannot spend all our time reading the Bible and books on religion and theology. We must also go into life where people are and be constantly alert to words, how they are used, and what they mean in the specific connotations of current usage. This is our special task as preachers. We must not only be translators of Greek and Hebrew, we must also be translators of ideas into the everyday words of the person in the street. If we are to do this we must be constantly aware that words are only symbols and as such they are constantly changing and taking on and losing fine shades of meaning.

Contractions are Orally Weak Words

Rudolf Flesch, in *The Art of Readable Writing*,[1] points out that if we are to write informal English it is essential that we use contractions. However, in the pulpit, contractions create a problem. Contractions are words which are slurred together and consequently offer a short cut in everyday conversation. When the contraction is used within the pulpit the clarity of the word is often affected with a resulting lack of carrying power and force. In the speaking situation a word like "can't" does not have the carrying power of the word "cannot," particularly when the "not" is given its full oral value by the speaker. The rule we would suggest, therefore, is to use the contraction with caution and never use it in those statements where the negative emphasis is essential to the structural continuity of ideas. For example, a key sentence (a sentence that carries the structural outline of the sermon) should never contain a contraction. If it is a question of being colloquial in our speaking but thereby running the danger of poor audibility, then we must choose oral clarity rather than literary informality.

The Problem of the Pronoun

Many pronouns, like contractions, are weak words in oral production. Pronouns are only mirrors of the real thing. A mirror reflects whatever is near it regardless of anything but the nearness of what it reflects. In oral production pronouns such as she, he, it, and they demand that the listeners, consciously or unconsciously, think back and remember what is being mirrored in the pronoun. When you speak, you want a person to think with you. There is no time for the listener to go back and relisten to what has been said. Either he stays with you or he is lost. Therefore, we should avoid, wherever possible, all words which demand backtracking thought. This can be overdone. We do not recommend the elimination of all personal pronouns, but they should be used sparingly. Remember that you may have something clearly in mind but your listener comes to each new statement you make without the advantage of the total thinking of your mind. Therefore, don't make listening difficult by rambling on and on using one personal pronoun after another until "he" could mean almost anyone mentioned in the last twenty sentences. The spoken word is far more elusive than the written word and the pronoun is one of the most elusive words of all in the act of communicating an idea.

"You" is the exception. This may seem like poor English but it is a very sound statement. The pronoun "you" is direct and personal; it requires no reflective action and leaves no doubt as to whom you are referring in the speaking situation. All great oral writing makes extensive use of the pronoun "you." It puts a sharp edge or point to your ideas and drives them home personally to the listener.

"We" is also a powerful word. It is direct and personal and has the additional advantage of developing rapport between the speaker and the listener. It is a means of avoiding the impression that you are talking *at* your listeners and helps to establish the feeling that you are talking *with* them. We should also add that, in many cases, it will help in our own spiritual development to remind ourselves that we are included as the target of God's saving and condemning Word.

Follow Every Abstract Word With a
Specific Example or a Concrete Illustration

Until John Locke's philosophical analysis of language no one really faced the fact that words are only symbols. Locke pointed out that words do not possess any natural connection with the things they signify. Because of this we can learn and use words that have for us no clear mental content whatever. Particularly is this true of abstract words. A preacher can stand in the pulpit and speak words such as justice, faith, and grace that are recognizable to his listeners but which communicate nothing. Therefore, it is important that we form the habit of defining terms. When we use an abstract word for the first time in the sermon, we should follow it with a concrete illustration or example. These illustrations generally fall into the classification of animated expressions such as metaphors and similes.

As was indicated in the beginning of this chapter, there is a trend to eliminate all so-called "professional" words, such as redemption, justification, and sanctification, from popular theological discussions. The argument is that they confuse the issue and create barriers between laypersons and the professionally trained theologians. To a great extent this is true; technical words can do just that. But, on the other hand, words are only symbols and there is nothing inherently wrong with a technical term. If words are clearly defined they will communicate no matter how specialized their meaning might be. If we, as preachers, follow the advice of current authorities and avoid all theological words in the pulpit, it seems to me that we shall be preventing our listeners from exploring the Scriptures and theological writing on their own. After all, the Scriptures and historical theological writings are filled with technical terms. If, on the other hand, we acquaint our people with theological language by the frequent use and explanation of it in the pulpit so that this language becomes a part of their vocabularies, we shall enable our laity to delve directly into the theological literature of all times and grow in their own understanding of God's Word.

The sermon should be a means by which laypersons grow intellectually as well as spiritually. Therefore, don't avoid professional words just because they are technical; rather, when necessary, use them challengingly, always remembering the teaching-preacher's responsibility to make the unknown clear by relating it to the known. This means that the first time an abstract theological term is used in the sermon it should be followed by a concrete illustration, a specific example, or a clear definition.

2. Words of Variety

Not only must the spoken word be clear and understandable, but in oral writing the spoken word must be attractive to the ear as well. Spoken words can be made orally attractive by their variety.

Language scholars tell us that the speaker has a mountain of about 200,000 words at his disposal. The average speaker can use about 120 words per minute. This means that 2,400 words will be spoken in a twenty minute sermon. The vocabulary of the average person is about 2,000 words, which means that one could exhaust his vocabulary in one sermon if it were not for the obvious fact that many words are used more than once. This still presents the sermon, however, as a real challenge to increase one's word power. There are several suggestions that will help develop variety in our use of words.

Build a Strong Speaking Vocabulary

The recommendation of "vocabulary builders" is that the addition of one word a day to the speaker's vocabulary would greatly increase his ability to express himself. They suggest that the speaker should become word conscious. When reading and listening to others speak, he should be observant to see how other people use words. When a new word is heard, a mental note should be made of it. If possible, the word should be written down. As soon as possible, the word should be used.

I would agree with this general advice of increasing one's vocabulary. However, I think there is a danger of becoming a word-sleuth and simply adding new words to one's speaking vocabulary for the sake of impressing listeners. As preachers of the Word we are interested in communication and many times the simple advice to add new words to a speaking vocabulary will not necessarily guarantee our ability to express ourselves more clearly.

To improve our ability to communicate, it is important that we realize that we have three definite vocabularies. One is the *recognition* vocabulary. These are the words that we recognize and understand when we see them in print. The second is the *recall* vocabulary. These are the words that we can recall and use if we make a special effort; but it takes time to think them out from the back of our minds. The third is our *usable and ready* vocabulary. These words are immediately accessible and flow forth as part of our expression of ideas without any conscious effort.

The first vocabulary, recognition, is the largest and most extensive. The second, recall, contains fewer words; and the third, ready words, contains the fewest of all. The task of increasing one's vocabulary for speech is the process of transferring words from one vocabulary to the other, taking words out of the recognition, bringing them through the recall stage and finally into the stage of ready and usable words. This is not just setting out to hunt new words, as much as it is making the words we already know and possess, in a limited form, ready and usable.

How is this accomplished? By writing, reading, and then writing and reading some more. Writing gives you the opportunity to think and recall. Reading reminds you constantly of the words you know. Much has already been said in this book concerning the value of writing the sermon in full for clarity and style. It should be added that writing increases your speaking vocabulary and enables you to use a greater variety of words. In the long run, this process of building your vocabulary by bringing words through the three stages of development — recognition, recall, and ready usability — will prove the most helpful for your sermon writing and delivery.

3. Words of Animation

An Arabian proverb says: "He is the best orator who can turn men's ears into eyes." To accomplish this, oral writing suggests the use of language that is pictorial. A picture, they say, is worth a thousand words, in oral writing an effective *word picture* is worth a thousand logical arguments. To achieve picturesque language in our writing, we would suggest words of *animation*.

Simile

One of the most common classifications of words that draw pictures is the simile. A simile is intended to stir our imaginations by comparing two things which are, in general, quite different but which have a certain point of resemblance. The comparison is expressed by the use of the words *like* and *as*.

One has only to turn to the Bible to find excellent examples of their use:

> *And the daughter of Zion is left*
> *like a booth in a vineyard*
> *like a lodge in a cucumber field*
> *like a besieged city.*
>
> *Isaiah 1:8*

> *Their arrows are sharp,*
> *all their bows are bent,*

their horses hoofs seem like flint
their wheels like the whirlwind.
Their roaring is like a lion,
like young lions they roar;
they growl and seize their prey,
they carry it off, and none can rescue.
They will growl over it on that day,
like the roaring of the sea.

Isaiah 5:28-30

This is great oral writing. It creates vivid pictures within the mind. It is preaching that never dies but comes with a freshness and a vitality and sets an example for effective preaching in every age. It is God's Word clothed in picturesque animated words that people cannot escape, but must face, and either accept or reject.

Metaphor

The second picture-builder is the metaphor which is an implied comparison. Metaphors differ from similes by the fact that they are not introduced by *like* or *as*. The simile states, *that is like this*; the metaphor states, *that is this.*

Here again the Bible possesses some excellent examples. Jeremiah speaks of "the sword devouring the prophets." Christ refers to his followers as "the salt of the earth" and "the light of the world." He speaks of himself as "the vine," "the door," "the light." These are implied comparisons. They are quick, vivid pictures, animated words that come forth like colorful designs on a canvas of truth, that seem to hang in the minds of people, continually reminding them of what our Lord has said. It is great oral writing and makes for effective preaching.

Contrast

The third picture builder is words of contrast. They are used to create miniature balanced statements. A word is made stronger by contrasting it with its opposite. For example, we speak of *life and death, heaven and hell, joy and pain.* Words, like colors, receive added brilliance by their surroundings, particularly when their surroundings are in contrast.

Personification

The fourth picture builder is personification. The advice to "put people into your sentences" should not stop with the human race. Animals have been used to convey ideas and add color to abstract concepts since Aesop wrote his fables. Personification doesn't even have to stop with animals. For who hasn't spoken to his car when it wouldn't start, or tongue-lashed a chair that stubbed a toe, or hit a door that wouldn't open? This is the most natural reaction of our relation to the inanimate world about us — to see life in lifeless things. This is an excellent technique for animating your writing and speaking.

Warning

It is important to note the dangers of using similes, metaphors, and personifications in sermon writing. Be careful to avoid mixed figures of speech. One good animated phrase is enough for any one idea. Use more and your writing will take on the aspects of a Picasso abstract. Also strive for freshness and avoid the trite, hackneyed examples of picturesque writing that are too commonly used. The effect of animated words is achieved by the element of surprise which enters into your choice of comparing two dissimilar things.

Slang

Many animated and picturesque words fall into the classification of slang. According to language scholars, slang originated as the secret code of tramps and thieves. For many critics it has never elevated its social standing. Others defend it as a striking and novel manner of speaking. The danger of using slang in the pulpit is that, if it is new and novel, few listeners will know what it means; if it is familiar to most, it is more than likely overworked and trite. Slang words, true to their linguistic origin, still remain primarily a secret code of the inner circle of the informed or they pass over into the classification of a cliche. If communication is to be our guide to effective writing, this should be reason enough to discourage the use of slang in the pulpit.

4. *Words of Beauty*

People are influenced and convinced not only by what is reasonable and visual, but also by what is agreeable and easy to listen to. Many times a person who has little to say, and says it well, is listened to; but the person who has much to say, and says it poorly, is ignored. Whether we approve of this or not, the fact remains that if we would stand before an audience today, even a fellowship of saints, we must speak attractively.

This does not necessarily mean that we are to tell funny little stories and sprinkle our sermons with pointless anecdotes. The question of whether or not humor has a place in the pulpit is answered graphically by the attempts of the average pastor to be funny. There are, however, exceptions to this advice. If you find a humorous, but appropriate story or incident to illustrate or support a point, by all means use it. The final test is always the illustration itself. Does it fit? The important thing to remember concerning humor is that it should never be considered as an *end* in itself. This means that you should never tell a story in the pulpit with the intention of getting a laugh. Strive to make your material attractive but never mere entertainment.

There are many appropriate techniques for adding interest and color to public address. The most important for the pulpit is the sheer appreciation of the beauty of the spoken word. Words should be evaluated for the beauty of their sound and the harmony which results when they are spoken with other words. To initiate your own exploration of attractive and beautiful words, we suggest the following starters.

Echoisms

Echoisms are words which are dramatic actions within themselves. They create their own communication in sound. Technically this is referred to as *onomatopoeia*, or, sometimes, "sound sense." These are words that people like to hear and are attracted to because of the musical and dramatic quality of the words. Words such as hiss, click, pop, and crash are not just symbols of sound, but are imitations of the very sounds they symbolize.

In addition to onomatopoeia, echoisms include those words which, when orally produced, can dramatize what they symbolize. For example, *soft* can be said softly, *fast* can be produced rapidly, and *slow* produced slowly. This is true of many words, such as harsh, kind, cruel, cold, and warm. Our language is full of colorful words that, if spoken with feeling — that is, with dramatic interpretation of their meaning — can become true echoisms which take ordinary words and, by skillful oral interpretation, make of them words of beauty. Such words, completely understood, correctly chosen, and skillfully produced, will add great richness and color to your sermons. They will make listening to your ideas a pleasure for your audience.

Word Harmony

A discussion of word beauty should also consider the relationship between word sounds. Words, like notes of music or colors, can be arranged harmoniously or they can be thrown together with a resounding clash. One form of arranging words harmoniously is called *alliteration*, which is the repetition of the same letter or sound in a group of words. James Stewart describes the crucifixion as "a deed determined, dared, and done." The repeating of one word after another that begins with the letter "d" is unusual and attracts attention. Such a sentence appeals to the natural rhythmic sense of the average listener. This is effective if used sparingly and, I should add, skillfully. Nothing is worse than a speaker who attempts to be over-poetic and sacrifices the sense and meaning of what he is saying, simply to sound artistic.

We have all read sermons that use alliteration to form the basic outline. James Stewart uses alliteration as a technique in his outline of a sermon entitled, "Why Be A Christian." His points are that the Christian life is (1) *Happier* than any other, (2) *Holier* than any other, (3) More *hopeful* than any other. [2] When an outline falls naturally into such a series of words, alliteration can give the sermon carrying power. The danger is that many preachers develop alliterations as an habitual pattern for all their sermons. Not only is this extremely tiring and monotonous, but in many cases exactness of content is sacrificed to force the outline into this established alliteration pattern.

To gain harmony of words in relation to one another in oral writing is not to consciously strive for alliteration, but simply to develop a sense of beauty for word sounds. As you write, speak the sentences orally and see if they "speak well." You can read words silently that are unharmoniously combined and experience no jarring sensation, but if you take the time to read them aloud, it is at once apparent that they are irritating, discordant, and harsh to the ear. Technically this depends upon the euphony and cadence of word relations. It is established by arranging similar sounds and accents at measured intervals. But to establish rules for such writing and then attempt to master them would demand more time and effort than the average pastor has at his disposal. All of us, however, can greatly improve the sense of beauty in our sermon writing by oral trial and error. Listen to the sound of what you have written. If it doesn't speak well, write it again, and again if necessary, until it does. In this way, develop good taste for oral sounds and then write to please yourself. You will find from experience that such time and effort are wisely spent. You will not only have something to say, but you will have written something that you *want* to say, because it can be said well.

Pulpit Proprieties

Before closing this chapter on words, and this particular section on the beauty of words, it is appropriate that we say a word concerning *pulpit proprieties* — the etiquette and protocol of certain words and their use in the pulpit.

We have already discussed slang, but there is another classification of words called *euphemisms*, which are developed from the desire to avoid harsh, blunt, even crude words in the pulpit. For the most part, the words which create euphemism are perfectly good words but are considered, by some, improper words in certain situations. Such words as sweat, belly, stink, and guts have no place in the pulpit, according to many people.

On the other hand, many authorities in the field of English language studies are quite definite in their dislike of softpedaling spontaneous communications of thought by euphemisms. They consider the use of euphemisms a false delicacy and a violation of natural expression. They recommend calling a spade a spade. All attempts to avoid the harsh words are labeled by one language scholar as "decadent affectation of super-sensitive victorianism." A mild example would be the preacher who avoids saying that a man has died and says instead, "He has joined the church triumphant."

The pulpit is no place to champion academic causes; on the other hand, the pulpit need not be the last to accept modern literary opinion and evaluation of what is good, acceptable English usage. Perhaps all we can say is that the pulpit proprieties must be finally decided by the individual pastor in the light of his own experience and knowledge of his congregation. For the sake of seminarians, two practical observations can be made.

First, face frankly the fact that words like belly, sweat, and guts lack beauty of sound and are considered crude words in polite public conversation. Recognize that they may shock some members of the congregation you are called to serve. There are times when the intention of the preacher is to shock his listeners by what he is saying. In such cases, I would advise using strong words courageously, with the knowledge that you do so on the best literary advice. The gospel is basically concerned with sin and there are occasions in your sermons when you must illustrate sin in all its naked, vivid reality. Anything less is an offense against our Lord who died because of sin's shocking reality. On the other hand, if your intention is not to shock, then it is best to avoid harsh and shocking words. Otherwise you will defeat the very point you are making by diverting the attention of your listeners away from what you are saying to the manner in which you are saying it.

The second bit of advice concerning pulpit proprieties is this: The amount of liberty which you have in the pulpit to say what you want to say in the way in which you want to say it depends, to a large extent, on *who you are*. The ratio of freedom differs greatly between a seminarian and an experienced pastor. Dr. Halford Luccock, for example, could preach a sermon on the text, Acts 8:20 (where Peter says, "Thy silver perish with thee") and entitle his sermon "To Hell With You and Your Money." He could do this because he was a **distinguished writer and preacher, an accepted pulpit** scholar, and a Christian gentlemen with years of consecrated service to his credit. If a young seminarian were to say the same thing in the pulpit, it would be considered flippant and crude, if not blasphemous. Remembering that "fools rush in where angels fear to tread," the best advice is to wait until you are an experienced preacher before you try anything "foolish" in the pulpit. And I should hasten to add, fools for Christ are in good company according to St. Paul. We need more courageous and foolish preaching in the pulpit to shock people out of their religious complacency, but let us wait until the mark of the cross is on our lives and the Word of God is entrenched firmly within our hearts.

9
Rewriting and Revision

It is often said that anything worth doing is worth doing well. It should follow in the art of sermon preparation that anything worth writing is worth revising. Rewriting takes time. Lacking the enthusiasm and power of new ideas rushing into the mind, rewriting is often toilsome and grueling. But rewriting is essential. As Robert Louis Stevenson said, "When I say writing, O, believe me, it is rewriting that I have chiefly in mind."

There are several suggestions which will make the task of revision and rewriting more helpful and more meaningful.

1. Let your work get cold. If possible, never begin the revision of material immediately after you have finished it. Put it aside and undertake another activity. Then, when the mind is refreshed, return to the sermon and its revision.

2. Record the sermon. The acid test of the sermon is how it sounds when it is spoken. Therefore, switch roles. Put yourself in the position of one who will hear your sermon. Become a critical listener.

3. Revise with a purpose. Listen to your sermon several times and each time have a definite purpose for listening. In general we would suggest the following:

The First Listening

First record the rough draft of the sermon and listen for the total effect and overall impression of the content. This will involve asking certain specific questions in various categories.

1. Thrust and Continuity
  (a) When you have listened to the sermon, can you

state in one or two sentences what the sermon actually said?

(b) Were there "key words and phrases" that helped to give unity to the sermon? Can you identify four or five words that would summarize the development of content?

(c) Was there a logical development of ideas? Could you follow it?

(d) Were there times when the sermon went off on an unnecessary tangent? Were there times when the sermon said something that sent you as a listener off on your own line of thinking?

(e) Did the sermon have movement? Were there times when you felt, "O.K., you made your point, now move on."?

After this first listening make elaborate notes of desired changes on the manuscript. But don't rewrite yet. Listen to the sermon for the second time.

The Second Listening

The following questions are suggested:

1. Introduction

(a) Did the introduction recognize you and address you as a listener? Or did it jump immediately into the material at hand?

(b) Did the introduction attract your attention? Did it mention one of your interests or concerns?

(c) Did the introduction really introduce the theme of the sermon? Was this immediately apparent or did you discover the relationship later on in the sermon?

(d) Did the introduction agree in mood with the rest of the sermon?

(e) Was the introduction too long?

(f) Was there a smooth transition into the text, or the first point of the sermon?

After hearing the introduction, make notes of suggested changes to be made on the manuscript.

Then listen to the body of the sermon. And ask the following questions:

2. The Body of the Sermon

(a) Were the main points of the development clear? Did each step of the sermon development unfold naturally into the next which followed it?

(b) Did the sermon make any statements that it did not support? Were the supporting materials believable, or did they seem forced?

(c) Was there good balance in the sermon between the various sections, points, or parts?

(d) Did the sermon ask any questions that it did not answer?

(e) Did the sermon move smoothly, or were there awkward spots?

(f) Did the sermon have a point of climax? Did the rest of the development flow to this point and from it? Makes notes of suggested changes on the manuscript.

3. Conclusion

(a) Were there any ideas in the conclusion which were not mentioned in the development of the body of the sermon? If so, make a notation on the manuscript to take them out and place them where they logically belong in the body.

(b) Were there pre-conclusions or were you prepared for the ending of the sermon?

(c) Did the sermon conclusion drive home the main ideas of the sermon effectively? Or did the sermon just seem to come to an end?

(d) Did the conclusion give a real sense of completeness to the sermon?

(e) Was the conclusion related to the introduction? Make necessary notations on the manuscript and then consider the illustrations.

4. Illustrations

(a) Were the illustrations valid? Did they really illustrate the points made?

(b) Were the illustrations varied?

(c) Were the illustrations adequate?

(d) What illustrations seem to stand out? Did they inform the listener and enforce the point made or did they replace it?

Now you are ready to rewrite the sermon for the first time. Take all the suggested notes for changes and revise the manuscript accordingly. When you have finished this, record the revised sermon. You are now ready for a third listening. You will, of course, listen to see if the changes you made improve the sermon where needed.

The Third Listening

During this listening you will want your manuscript in front of you. The recorder should be placed near enough so that you can stop it when you need to make changes on the manuscript. This time, instead of rewriting the entire manuscript, you will make only small changes here and there. Start the recorder. Remember, the moment you hear something that doesn't sound right, stop the machine and correct the problem word or phrases.

1. Where can unnecessary words, phrases, and sentences be eliminated to increase the movement of content?

2. Do you use the same word over and over again in the space of a few sentences? If so, find a synonym that would work. A good thesaurus will help at this point.

3. Are the words fresh and clear?

4. Where is there need for an additional simile or metaphor?

5. Are there any words that sound awkward when spoken together? For example, the phrase "Christ's Cross" is a good written phrase but when produced

orally it is extremely awkward and difficult to say. Better to change it to "the Cross of Christ."

6. Are there too few or too many alliterations?

7. Listen for any way in which you can improve the listening quality of the sermon. Where does it not "speak well"?

The Fourth Listening

Now that you have made these changes on the manuscript, record the sermon again. Then listen to it for the fourth time. If there are minor changes to be made, make them.

You are now ready to write the sermon in its final form that you will carry into the pulpit.

If you take your sermon through these revisions and recordings and the four listening sessions, you will not only improve the content of the sermon but you will at the same time have familiarized yourself with the content of the sermon.

The unique appearance of the oral style manuscript, each page being different, will enable you to simply glance at a page and the very shape of the words placed upon it will remind you of the content contained on that page. The circled words, the underlined phrases, the oral markings will recall ideas of content easily to mind. With the exception of key sentences and perhaps transition sentences, you will not have to follow the manuscript word-for-word with your eyes, but you will produce the sermon using the same words and sentences used to write the sermon. This will be true only if you have developed your own personal oral style format.

10

Body Speech
Some Brief Notes on Delivery

The speaker is not just a voice, but a body. When we speak we do not simply use our vocal chords, lips, teeth, tongue, and lungs, but our total body. Therefore, speaking is "body speech." Our eyes, facial expressions, hands and arms, feet and legs all contribute to the art of speaking effectively.

The listeners are not only hearers, they are seers. The communication they receive from the pulpit is the total impact of a person addressing them with a message. Therefore, everything we do in the pulpit is as important as what we say.

Attitude

We began our discussion of preaching with the consideration of attitude. When we enter the pulpit, attitude is of primary importance both for contact and delivery. A listening congregation will forgive almost anything if they like the speaker as a person. There are two basic aspects to a winning pulpit personality:

1. A Good Attitude Toward the Task of Preaching and the Content of the Message. This is accomplished by conveying two impressions:

(a) *Happiness.* You should give the impression that you enjoy what you are doing. You should not rush into the pulpit giving the impression that you want to get in, get it over, and get out as soon as possible.

(b) *Confidence.* You should give the impression that you have thoroughly prepared your material. You know the subject you are talking about, and are convinced that it is important and interesting.

2. *A Good Attitude Toward the Listeners.* This is accomplished by conveying that you are:

(a) *Natural.* You are yourself in the pulpit. You are not trying to make a sale, and are not overly-aggressive or antagonistic toward the listeners. You should give the impression that you want to share yourself and your message with the listeners.

(b) *Pastoral.* You should give the impression that you are sincerely interested in the listeners, and are genuinely concerned for them. The listeners should feel that you are a kind and thoughtful person to whom they could take their problems and not be condemned but understood.

(c) *Friendly.* You should give the impression that you are not only interested and concerned for the listeners, but that you like them as well. You should not be authoritarian or condescending in your attitude. You should not give the impression that you are talking *at* them, or *down* to them, but *with* them.

Poise

Poise is the impression a speaker makes in the pulpit. It depends on three things:

1. Comfort. If you are to possess good poise in the pulpit, you must feel comfortable in it. This depends on the size and the design of the pulpit, which in most cases is fixed before we are called to it. But there are some things that can be done.

(a) If the pulpit desk is adjustable, make sure that it is at *the right height* for your sermon notes or manuscript, so that you may glance down with your eyes to see your notes without lowering your head.

If the desk is not adjustable, two things might be done. A wooden desk might be made to fit on top of the present desk and raise it to the desired height. Or a platform might be built in the floor of the pulpit to raise the speaker to the right height. This may seem an unnecessary concern, but I assure you that no person can preach his best unless he feels comfortable in the pulpit.

The pulpit desk should also have a lip to hold notes and manuscript from sliding to the floor.

(b) The *sides of the pulpit* should permit the speaker to rest his hands on the top-piece of the sides of the pulpit with the arms just slightly bent. This gives freedom for gesturing.

(c) The desk of the pulpit should be *adequately lighted* from above. No pulpit lamp should interfere, or project itself, between the speaker and the listeners.

2. *Control.* Control of the pulpit is completely within the jurisdiction of the speaker. It should not be approached as a barrier behind which the preacher is forced to speak. It should be viewed and used as a tool. Just as a tennis player uses his racket, or a golfer his clubs, the pulpit can be used by the preacher. When you want to become confidential, lean forward on the desk. When you desire to give a casual remark, lean against the side of the pulpit. When you change from one major idea to another, move slightly to one side of the pulpit. If you are talking about something sliding along, slide your hand along the top edge of the pulpit. Occasionally, for emphasis, strike the pulpit. Don't pound on it continuously, but use it when you think it is needed. The important thing is your own attitude toward the pulpit. Don't be afraid of it. Don't consider it a wall but an aide. With practice, the pulpit can become a part of you as a speaker and greatly contribute to the overall impression you make as you preach.

3. *Composure.* Composure is the control of the body in the pulpit. It is what we generally mean when we say poise. You should not be stiff or sloppy, but natural.

When you are in the pulpit you present a silhouette. If this silhouette does not change or move, it can have a negative effect upon the listeners. The eyes tire when what they are looking at, for any length of time, does not move. Like the concentration of the mind on content, the eyes focused on the speaker need rest. And we rest the viewing concentration of the listeners when we move.

Here are some do's and dont's about movement in the pulpit:

(1) *Move for a reason.* There are many times during the sermon when movement of the body can be a gesture. When you change an idea or are showing a contrast, you can move from one side of the pulpit to the other. When you desire to be more confidential, you can move forward. When you are looking at an overall view of something, or are talking about perspective, you can move backward. Of course, all of these movements are slight. You are confined to a limited space in the pulpit. But because you are in the focus of the listener's attention, any movement, no matter how small, will be noticed.

(2) *Avoid rocking from side to side in the pulpit.* This is easily solved. All you have to do is place one foot in front of the other, and you will not rock. Try it. If you start to rock, you will lose your balance immediately.

(3) *Avoid rocking back and forth, or up and down on your toes.* This is not as easily overcome as rocking from side to side, but placing one foot in front of the other will help.

(4) *Don't lean on the pulpit constantly.* This is a good gesture when the subject matter calls for it. But if you constantly lean on the desk, it loses its effectiveness as a gesture.

(5) *Don't "surfboard" the desk.* This is placing one hand on either side of the pulpit desk, and then leaning back as you hold on. Some speakers "surfboard" the pulpit desk through the entire sermon. This is not only annoying to the listeners, but also prohibits the use of the hands for gesturing.

(6) *Be careful how you hold your head*. The head can be used to gesture, but be careful not to let the bearing of the head become an attitude of your total poise in the pulpit. For example, the head slightly cocked to one side or the other gives a "cute" appearance. The chin slightly raised and jutting forward gives an impression of superiority. The head lowered and looking over the top of the glasses, gives a pseudo-intellectual appearance. Therefore, keep the bearing of the head natural. Above all do not emphasize each important word with a nod of the head.

(7) *Avoid all nervous movements and mannerisms*. The most common are playing with glasses, watch, rings; pulling your neck out of your collar; wringing or folding your hands. The problem here is that most of us are totally unaware of our mannerisms. Therefore, it is necessary to have someone make a note of them and inform you of those that are serious enough to distract attention while you are preaching.

Eye Contact

The eyes are the real point of contact with the listeners. The proper use of the eyes depends on facial mobility which is the facility of the face to respond to thoughts and feelings behind it. Therefore, our attitude is essential in the right use of the eyes. As we have mentioned before, the speaker should enter the pulpit with the attitude, "God loves you, and so do I." Take time to survey the congregation. Look to the front, the center, the back, and to the side sections of the congregation. Give the impression that you want to include everyone in the experience of sharing your message.

The key to good eye contact is *directness*. When you are delivering the sermon watch the reactions of your listeners. Try to make everyone in the audience feel that they are being singled out and talked to. This will mean not letting your eyes wander about the congregation, but have definite points at which you establish contact. You will discover that when you look at a certain section of people, everyone in that particular section will feel that you are talking directly to them. Sometimes it is helpful to pick out friendly and responsive faces. Talk to them. It will help to establish directness, and it will also help you as a speaker to receive the encouragement a friendly face can give.

The listener is conscious of the direction in which you are looking. So when you look down at the manuscript, never look back up at the same people. Change the direction of your eye contact when you look up from the manuscript. You will find that the people will think that you looked away from them not to view your manuscript, but in order that you might look at someone else in the congregation.

Gestures

Gestures are a natural part of conversational expression, but they are the most difficult activity of the body for the beginning speaker to master. This is true because gesturing is an unconscious activity. We gesture without thinking about it, and therefore the moment that we become conscious of our gestures, we either stop gesturing or produce gestures that are mechanical and artificial. There are several things that need to be said about the development of good gestures.

1. *The Physical Aspects of Gesturing.* In most cases we use our hands to gesture. Therefore, they should be free. Hands that are constantly gripping the pulpit or are in a folded position are not free to move. The movement of the hands originates, for the speaker, at the elbows. When the movement originates at the shoulders, the gestures are over-exaggerated. When the wrists originate the movement, the gestures are weak and effeminate. It is the elbows that need to be free and flexible, if the hands are to operate effectively.

2. *There Are Various Types of Hand Gestures.* The two most common types are the emphatic and the descriptive gestures.

(a) *The emphatic gesture* adds emphasis to what is being said. It generally consists of three steps: the *approach,* which is the outward movement of the hand; the *hit* which is the point of contact; and the *return,* which is withdrawing the hand to the original position. The important thing to remember is that the *approach* should not be too sudden or quick (unless your intention is to startle and surprise the listener with the gesture). The *hit* should occur at the same time as the word to be emphasized. Timing here is absolutely essential. Nothing is so distracting and even ridiculous in the pulpit than when the *hit* of an emphatic gesture occurs before or after the word to be emphasized. The *return* should also be easy and smooth, and not quick. Don't jab your listeners with gestures.

(b) Then there are *descriptive gestures.* These help to create a picture for the listeners. You actually draw in the air what you are talking about. Students have found it helpful to practice such gesturing by taking a pencil and piece of paper, and while going over the sermon, doodle with the pencil. Or if there is a chalkboard handy, they speak the sermon to the chalkboard and draw descriptive designs to indicate what they are talking about. This teaches the mind the co-ordination between hands and voice.

Many descriptive gestures do not have to be complete drawings. They can be suggestive movements, such as the swish of the hand to indicate speed, or the drawing of the hands apart to indicate separation.

The type and degree of gesturing depends totally on the content of the message. Gestures are meant to reinforce what is being said, not as a substitute for what the speaker fails to say. No amount of beating on the pulpit will make a weak point strong. It will only exaggerate the apparent lack of support for the idea.

This means that the more exciting, descriptive, and valid the content, the more gestures are needed.

Many beginning speakers are afraid of gestures because they have heard so often the put down, "He couldn't speak without his hands." Therefore, they become overly conscious of gesturing. Remember that when gestures are used well, the listeners are not aware of them. Therefore, if gestures are well done, they can never be overdone.

3. How Do You Develop Good Gestures? As most of you know from experience, this is not easy because gesturing is an unconscious process. The best way to develop good gestures is to first *observe* good gestures. And second, *teach the unconscious mind* the necessity of good gesturing.

(a) *Observe.* No one can produce a gesture that he has never seen. Every gesture we use is by the process of imitating someone else. We are not conscious of this, but it is true nevertheless. Therefore, make it a practice to watch effective speakers with the specific intention of noticing how they gesture. Also watch people in everyday conversational situations. See how they use their hands to convey meaning and emphasize what they are saying.

(b) *Teach the unconscious mind the importance of good gesturing.* The problem is that we look at people using gestures and never really see the gestures because we are concentrating on what is being said. Therefore, watch people gesture and concentrate on the gestures. Tell your unconscious mind, "Look at that gesture. Learn it. And when I am speaking in the pulpit, direct my hands to produce that gesture." This advice may sound strange. I am not enough of a psychologist to explain how or why this works. But the long experience of teaching students to speak and gesture assures me that it really does work.

One of the best ways to teach the unconscious mind the art of good gesturing is to practice telling a descriptive story and use all the gestures you can to animate it, at the same time being conscious of what you are doing with your hands. It is as if you tell your unconscious mind, "Now watch this." For example, tell about how a person puts a coin in the Coke machine. (Show how he does it with your own hands.) Then tell how he opens the bottle. (Demonstrate this with your hands.) Then tell that he puts another coin in the snack machine. (Demonstrate that as you tell it.) Then he opens the sack of peanuts. (Move your hands as if you were opening the sack.) Then show how he pours the peanuts into the bottle and shakes it up. (Do that.) Finally, show how he drinks the mixture. Now tell the story without descriptive hand gestures. Then tell it again with gestures. This will help convince both you and your unconscious mind how effective the important gestures are. It will also make you a better teller of stories to your friends.

Voice

The voice is vital to good speaking. If you have been endowed with an excellent speaking voice, you are fortunate. If not, you can always improve the voice you have.

1. Projection. No matter what you have to say, or how well you express it, all will be in vain unless the listeners are able to hear it. There are several things that can be said about projection.

(a) Projection, like gesturing, is basically an *unconscious process.* When I am talking face-to-face with a person my voice automatically adjusts to the intimate situation. I do not think I must lower my voice and adjust my vocal mechanism to produce an intimate tone. No. It just happens. When, on the other hand, I see a person across the campus, I shout at him. I do not have to think about increasing volume; it just happens. Why? Because the eyes send a message to the unconscious mechanisms of speech and the process occurs automatically. The eyes, therefore, are essential for good projection. Caruso reportedly told his students that he always sang to the last row in the balcony. This is good advice. A speaker should always adjust his voice to the size of the room. That means speaking to the last row of the congregation. And that means looking back there occasionally to maintain the correct level of projection.

(b) The *eyes of the listeners* are also important to insure adequate projection. Listeners, as we have said, not only listen to a voice, they watch a speaker. They read lips and facial expressions as well as gestures. Therefore, the movement of the speaker's lips and facial gestures affect the quality of projection.

(c) Projection is not only determined by volume, it is also effected by *rate, pronunciation, and articulation.* Many times people say that they didn't hear the speaker. The truth is they heard well enough the sounds the speaker was making — the volume was loud enough — but they could not identify the sounds they heard. The sounds they heard were muffled or scrambled together and did not form recognizable words.

2. *Rate.* No one speaks too fast if he can be heard and understood. Rate varies with the speaker. But there are several general comments that can be helpful.

(a) Rate depends a great deal on the *material* that is being communicated. Descriptions and unimportant statements can be produced more rapidly. "Key sentences" and important statements that carry a main thought or an important idea should be produced more deliberately.

(b) Rate depends not only on the *pause between words spoken,* but it also depends on the *elongation of vowel sounds.* Often the speaker gives the impression that he is speaking too fast because he fails to give full value to vowel sounds, not because he is producing too many words per minute. The clarity of speech depends on consonants, but the richness and the quality of the human voice is produced by the vowel tones. Therefore, correct rate is maintained not only by giving full value to vowel tones, but the quality of the voice is improved. Do not slight vowel sounds. Give them their full rounded tones.

(c) The *size of the room* also determines rate. The farther words must travel to reach the listeners, the more individual words need to be separated. For as words travel in space, they tend to move closer together.

3. Pronunciation. Pronunciation is uttering words with correct vowel and consonant sounds, correct division of syllables, and correct accent. Here the speaker should make use of the dictionary or some special aids such as Richard C. White's book, *The Vocabulary of the Church.*

4. Articulation. Mispronouncing words is the unpardonable sin of the public speaker. You may mispronounce a word because you have always heard it mispronounced, and do not know the correct pronunciation. But poor articulation is sheer carelessness and laziness. Pronunciation is the correctness of a word. Articulation is the distinctness of the word. Poor articulation is the result of laziness of the vocal mechanism. We are lazy about getting our mouths open, our lips moving, and using our tongues on lips and teeth to produce correct sounds.

Here are a few of the most common errors of articulation heard in our seminary chapel:

(a) The word *just* becomes "jist." This is by far the most common fault. Over ninety percent of the speakers in our chapel are guilty of this.

(b) The word *for* becomes "fer." This is true not only when the word is used by itself, but also when it forms part of another word, such as *forgiveness*. It becomes "fergiveness."

(c) The *ing* sound on the endings of words becomes "en." For example, *coming* and *going* become "comen" and "goen."

(d) The *ness* sound at the endings of words becomes "niss." For example, *forgiveness* becomes "forgiveniss." Then if the *for* syllable is also faulty the compounded results are "fergiveniss."

(e) A common fault is to drop the *g* sound in the word "strength" so that it becomes "strenth."

(f) Words which possess the *en* sound frequently become "in." For example, *men* becomes *min*. And likewise the vowel *a* becomes an *e*. For example, *many* and *any* become "meny" and "eny."

(g) When a word which ends with a consonant is used before a word beginning with a consonant, the last consonant of the first word is dropped. For example, the statement, "God did it," becomes "Gaw did it."

Many more faults could be mentioned. But if the average speaker avoided just those seven faults he would greatly improve his articulation in the pulpit. There is really no excuse for poor articulation. It can easily be corrected with determination and practice. Ask a friend to listen to you preach and make notes of your faulty articulation. Then set about correcting your most common faults. The improvement this will bring will be well worth the time and effort.

General Comments

1. *Nervousness.* Nervousness is nothing more than uncontrolled energy. And energy is an absolute necessity for effective speaking. It is a gift of our physical nature. When primitive man was confronted with a wild beast, the adrenalin flowed and produced the extra energy needed to protect himself. When you face the public spotlight of the pulpit, the adrenalin flows and

you are given extra energy, not to protect yourself but to *project* yourself better in the speaking situation. Therefore, don't fear nervousness; be thankful for it and use it. Learn to control it; it's what you need. Never try to eliminate it. You will find that if you use your total body energetically in the pulpit this nervousness will be the very thing you need to put your whole self into the sermon.

2. *Imitation.* There are two ways to learn to speak effectively — experience and observation. Experience will come with opportunities. Observation needs to be a developed skill. You can never produce a sound you have not heard and you can never produce a gesture you have not seen. Therefore, listen and watch talented speaking personalities, and learn from them. Never imitate one particular speaker, but study skillful speakers and learn how they do it. Then be selective. No speaker is perfect. Learn what a particular speaker's strong points are, and then develop a style of your own that is a combination of the best qualities you have observed and learned.

The speaker is a body and when you speak your whole body speaks. The listener is a see-er as well as a hearer and the message he receives is from the total personality of the speaker. This is "body speech."

APPENDIX
EXAMPLES OF ORAL STYLE FORMAT

The following examples of oral style format were chosen to illustrate the many variations in appearance and style which result when the individual student puts into practice the art of oral writing.

Because each preacher must discover by trial and error the type of format that best serves him in the pulpit, we present the examples without editing to make them conform with the specific suggestions given in this book.

Example One is average. Imporant words are circled; words to be stressed are underlined; and indentation is used to show the relationship of word groupings to each other. Lines drawn across the page indicate separate ideas. This page of the sermon manuscript deals with the fifth point of the sermon. The triple lines indicate that a new point follows. Other oral markings are difficult to translate but they mean something to the author of the sermon and that is all that matters.

EXAMPLE ONE

"My sheep (HEAR) me."

"I (KNOW) my sheep."
"*My sheep* follow (ME.)"

"*I give* my sheep (ETERNAL LIFE.)"

And |finally| then *Christ answers* with the (GREATEST PROMISE OF ALL)
   "NO ONE SHALL SNATCH MY SHEEP OUT OF MY HAND."

This is the (ROCK of our HOPE) —

   on which ALL FAITH is BUILT.

Not the SANDY FOUNDATIONS of

CONDITIONS —

   which must be met by our |MORAL

      |and ETHICAL

         |EFFORTS.

" IF YOU DO THIS

THEN GOD WILL DO THAT "

If you are| GOOD

   | and FAITHFUL

      | and LOVING

| and TRUSTWORTHY —

(if) you GRAB HOLD of GOD

and NEVER LET GO

\THEN/— you will BE SAVED!

(NO!) Christ is saying here —

(GOD) GRABS HOLD of US

and (HE) WILL ** NEVER ** LET ** GO!

and \NOTHING

and \NOBODY SHALL SNATCH US

FROM (THE GRIPPING HAND OF GOD!!!)

Example Two is similar to example one; the important words are circled and the words to be stressed are underlined, but here we see the use of cartoons and symbols. They give a distinctive individuality to the page and suggest the content to the preacher. Note that key words are written in the margin to suggest the main subjects dwelt with on this page.

EXAMPLE TWO

This you see is the [MEANING] and the [PURPOSE] of LENT

MEANING
↓
PURPOSE

LENT is the [SEASON] when we as the CHURCH

[HOLD] [UP] [THE] [CROSS] [OF] [CHRIST] — ANEW!!

and (call) to every MAN, WOMAN, and CHILD

to [LOOK TO THIS CROSS!!]

(NOT) an EMPTY CROSS —

but a CROSS whereon [HANGS] our [CRUCIFIED] [LORD.]

We call upon all people — (as well as ourselves)

to look at those [NAIL PIERCED HANDS

HANDS
SIDE
BROW

that [SPEAR TORN SIDE

the [THORN CROWNED BROW

See the spittle of [MAN'S MOCKERY] —

running down the [FACE] of a [FORGIVING

[GOD:]

BUT (MORE) —

LOOK into the [EYES OF CHRIST]

those eyes of [COMPASSION.

|FORGIVENESS

and|LOVE.

Look LONG and WELL and REMEMBER

though we again and again

TAKE OUR EYES OFF OF HIM

HE NEVER TAKES HIS EYES OFF OF

US!!!

REMEMBER!

HIS
EYES

Example three contains no circled words or underlined phrases. All letters are capitalized and the format is quite open. The use of periods at the place of pauses is an example of individual style. The student says that it helps while he is in the process of writing and indicates a certain hesitancy that he feels at this particular point. The periods convey to him a feeling about the content of this page. This is an illustration of the complete freedom which the writer has in oral writing to put down anything on the page he desires — anything that will help him. Consciously or unconsciously the student associates certain reactions to these markings and therefore they have a most important role to play in oral writing even though to the observer they make no sense whatsoever.

EXAMPLE THREE

WE PROHIBIT THE CHURCH . . . THE BODY OF CHRIST . . .

FROM BEING PRECISELY WHAT CHRIST INTENDED IT TO BE . . .

THE SEEKING . . . SEARCHING . . .

SWEEPING . . .

INSTRUMENT OF GOD'S LOVE

IN A LOVELESS . . .

LOST . . .

SINFUL . . .

WORLD!!!!!

NO . . . JESUS WANTS . . . NOT A GRUMBLING . . . BICKERING . . .

ANTAGONISTIC . . . SELF-CENTERED . . .

BLIND . . . CHURCH!!

HE DEMANDS . . . A REJOICING CHURCH . . .

A PEOPLE WHO REJOICE WITH GOD . . .

OVER ONE LIFE RESTORED TO ITS

FULL DIGNITY!!!

HE WANTS A SYMPATHETIC CHURCH . . .

WHICH TAKES THE INITIATIVE . . . AND .

GO OUT . . . AND LOOK!!!

A PEOPLE WHO WILL SUPPORT AND BACK UP . . .

EVERY EFFORT . . . TO RESTORE HUMAN DIGNITY!!!!

Example Four is an illustration of a format where the writer has combined the full manuscript with an outline. The resulting format is most interesting, but very time-consuming to write. It enables the speaker to follow the outline when he desires or where necessary refer to the complete wording of his idea. Many students complete their entire manuscript and then write outline words in the margin as they are in the process of familiarizing themselves with the sermon. (This is also done in example two in the right hand margin.) They say that a quick glance at the key word enables them to recall what they have written in full at this point of the manuscript.

EXAMPLE FOUR

WORLDLY
MEN

WORLDLY MEN are like ATH-
LETES in a stadium

they practice self-control,

they exert themselves

they face dangers,

ONE WINS
PRIZE

And only one receives the prize.
The others

get NOTHING.

IRONY

even more ironic

is the fact
that this prize is perishable.

IVY LEAVES

It is like a wreath of ivy leaves

which withers away and dies.

The earth is full of such people —

WORDLY PEOPLE

They live only in the stadium of space

and time.

STADIUM

They work and strive only for things—

that are SEEN.

They compete for PRIZES

LOSS

which can only be gained at another's

LOSS.

Their prizes either RUST

or BURN

or ROT away —

and they are gone.

BOXERS

These people are like boxers

who aimlessly flay the air.

The testimony of the students represented by these examples is that the oral style format which they use has greatly aided them in making their preaching more effective. The important thing is that the style of the format must be the individual creation of the preacher. There are no limitations to this creativity.

NOTES

CHAPTER 2
1. James Cleland, *The True and Lively Word* (New York, Charles Scribner's Sons, 1954).
2. Yngve Brilioth, *A Brief History of Preaching* (Philadelphia, Fortress Press, 1965).

CHAPTER 3
1. David Redding, *The Miracles of Christ* (New Jersey, Fleming H. Revell Company, 1964), p. 95.
2. Fenelon, *Dialogues on Eloquence*, trans. Wilbur Howell (Princeton, Princeton University Press, 1951), p. 111.

CHAPTER 4
1. Paul Sherer, *For We Have This Treasure* (New York, Harper and Brothers, 1944), p. 178-179.
2. Aurelius Augustine, De Doctrina Christiana, In: Philip Schaff, ed., *A Select Library of the Nicene and Post Nicene Fathers of the Church*, Vol. II (New York

CHAPTER 5
1. Quintilian, *Institutes of Oratory*, Book X.
2. Paul Sherer, *op. cit.*, p. 178.
3. Robert J. MacCracken, *The Making of the Sermon* (New York, Harper and Brothers, 1956), p. 71.
4. George Buttrick, *Jesus Came Preaching* (New York, Charles Scribner's Sons, 1951), p. 163.
5. Charlton Laird, *The Miracle of Language* (Cleveland, World Publishers, 1960).
6. Wilfred Funk, "There Ain't Nothing Wrong with Ain't," *The American Weekly*.
7. Walt Whitman, *Slang in America*, in: Ernest Sandeen, Ego in New Eden, *American Classics Reconsidered* (New York, Charles Scribner's Sons, 1958), p. 234.
8. Webb Garrison, *The Preacher and His Audience* (Westwood, N.J., Fleming H. Revell Co., Inc., 1954), p. 97.

9. Henry Sloan Coffin, in: *Here Is My Method*, Donald Macleod, ed. (Westwood, N.J., Fleming H. Revell Co., Inc., 1952), p. 58-59.

CHAPTER 7

1. Unpublished sermon, R. C. Hoefler.
2. Edmund Steimle, *Are You Looking for God?* (Philadelphia, Muhlenberg Press, 1957), p. 142.
3. David Woodyard, *Living Without God Before God* (Philadelphia, Westminster Press, 1968), p. 30.
4. James Stewart, *The Strong Name* (New York, Charles Scribner's Sons, 1941), p. 55.
5. Arthur John Gossip, *Experience Worketh Hope* (New York, Charles Scribner's Sons, 1945), p. 24.
6. *ibid.*, p. 5.
7. *ibid.*, p. 3.
8. *ibid.*, p. 30.
9. *ibid.*, p. 34.
10. *ibid.*, p. 41.
11. *ibid.*, p. 79.
12. Edmund A. Steimle, *op. cit.*, p. 130.
13. Helmut Thielicke, *The Waiting Father* (New York, Harper and Brothers, 1959), p. 136.
14. Edmund A. Steimle, *op. cit.*, p. 139.
15. David Redding, *op. cit.*, p. 127.
16. *ibid.*, p. 137.
17. *ibid.*, p. 27.
18. Edmund A. Steimle, *op. cit.*, p. 139.
19. Peter Marshall, *Mr. Jones Meet the Master*, (Westwood, N. J., Fleming H. Revell Co., Inc., 1950), p. 86.
20. Dr. Lenski, unpublished lectures on preaching, Preaching Institute of the U.L.C.A., 1959.
21. Unpublished sermon, R. C. Hoefler.
22. Arthur John Gossip, Op. Cit., p. 8.
23. *ibid.*, p. 11.
24. *ibid.*, p. 83.
25. Helmut Thielicke, op. cit., p. 82.

CHAPTER 8

1. Rudolf Flesh, *The Art of Readable Writing* (New York, Collier Books, 1962), p. 96-98.
2. James S. Stewart, *The Gates of New Life* (New York, Charles Scribner's Sons, 1940), p. 21-31.